God and Government

Other books by Gary DeMar:

God and Government
Issues in Biblical Perspective

God and Government
The Restoration of the Republic

Ruler of the Nations

Surviving College Successfully: A Complete
Manual for the Rigors of Academic Combat

The Reduction of Christianity
A Biblical Response to Dave Hunt (with Peter Leithart)

Something Greater Is Here

The Debate over Christian Reconstruction

The Legacy of Hatred Continues (with Peter Leithart)

"You've Heard it Said": 15 Biblical Misconceptions
that Render Christians Powerless

War of the Worldviews
A Christian Defense Manual

America's Christian History: The Untold Story

To Pledge Allegiance
A New World in View (with Fred Douglas Young)

Last Days Madness
Obsession of the Modern Church

To Pledge Allegiance
From Reformation to Colonization (with Fred Douglas Young and Gary Todd)

Volume I

God and Government

A Biblical and Historical Study

Gary DeMar

AMERICAN VISION, INC.

Atlanta, Georgia

God and Government: A Biblical and Historical Study is produced by American Vision, a Christian educational and communications organization. American Vision publishes a monthly magazine, *Biblical Worldview*, which is edited by Gary DeMar. For more information about American Vision and how to obtain a subscription to *Biblical Worldview* and receive a catalog of materials, write:

American Vision
P.O. Box 220
Powder Springs, Georgia 30127
or call 1–800–628–9460.

American Vision web site: www.americanvision.org

Unless otherwise noted, all Scripture quotations are taken from the *New American Standard Version* of the Bible. Copyright © The Lockman Foundation 1960, 1962, 1963, 1968, 1971, 1972, 1973, 1975, 1977, 1995. Used by permission.

ISBN: 0–915815–09–5 (Volume 1)
ISBN: 0–915815–15–X (3 volume set)

Text and photo acquisition by Gary DeMar

Art Direction by Diane Hosch

Series Design by Erin Sherman

Dedication and Acknowledgments

This first volume of *God and Government* is dedicated to a man of humble and generous spirit whose faithful support has made possible the educational program of American Vision. His example of Christian commitment is an encouragement for everyone who desires to see America returned to the solid foundation of God's Word. This Christian gentleman, who desires to remain anonymous, illustrates the truth of Matthew 20:26: "Whoever wishes to become great among you shall be your servant." His attitude of humble service in the advancement of Christ's kingdom is an inspiration to God's people everywhere not to "lose heart in doing good, for in due time we shall reap if we do not grow weary" (Galatians 6:9).

I would like to express my appreciation to the American Vision staff for their dedication in seeing this work completed: Jenny Venable for her speedy and accurate typing; Collie Owens for his invaluable editorial assistance; and Erin Sherman for the layout and design. I would also like to express my appreciation to Christine Kline who spent many hours editing the manuscript and to Archie Jones who provided many bibliographical and historical insights.

President George Washington issued the first Thanksgiving Proclamation under the new Constitution on October 3, 1789. He stated: *It is the duty of all Nations to acknowledge the providence of Almighty God, to obey his will, to be grateful for his benefits, and humbly to implore his protection and favor.* He went on to proclaim that there should be a day of *thanks-giving and prayer to be observed by acknowledging with grateful hearts the many signal favors of Almighty God, especially by affording them an opportunity peaceably to establish a form of government for their safety and happiness.*

Contents

Signing of the Mayflower Compact aboard the Mayflower in 1620: *In the name of God, Amen. We, whose names are underwritten, the loyal subjects of our dread sovereign lord King James, by the grace of God, of Great Britain, France, and Ireland, king, defender of the faith, etc., having undertaken for the glory of God and advancement of the Christian faith, and the honor of our king and country, a voyage to plant the first colony in the northern parts of Virginia; do by these presents, solemnly and mutually in the presence of God and one another, covenant and combine ourselves together into a civil body politic, for our better ordering and preservation and furtherance of other ends aforesaid; and by virtue hereof do enact, constitute and frame such just and equal laws, ordinances, acts, constitutions and offices, from time to time, as shall be thought most [suitable] and convenient for the general good of the colony; unto which we promise all due submission and obedience.*

Foreword

The Bible tells us that where there is no vision there is little, if any, future. A necessary ingredient in establishing a vision is the recognition of historical roots. To Americans this means a return to the biblical foundation that undergirded early America and that has given form and content to our freedoms. Gary DeMar's study is important for the simple fact that he calls us back to our historical and biblical moorings—moorings that are essential for future liberty.

Mr. DeMar emphasizes the biblical perspective in relation to the historical perspective. He begins with the question: "What does the Bible say about God and government?" From there, he analyzes the entire historical and governmental process according to the teachings of the Bible. This factor sets this work apart from others.

A return to the Bible as the foundation of American government is essential. In *How Should We Then Live?* (1976), Francis Schaeffer writes: "To whatever degree a society allows the teaching of the Bible to bring forth its natural conclusions, it is able to have form and freedom in society and government." Schaeffer goes on to note that with the loss of biblical absolutes in American culture, American society has become ripe for an authoritarian state.

Americans must again study the nature of their civil government. They must know why our society remains today the freest on the earth. Simply put, we must learn the lessons of history, or we are bound to repeat its failures.

The nineteenth century philospher Georg Wilhelm Friedrich Hegel once said: "History teaches us that man learns nothing from history." We must prove Hegel wrong. That is why Mr. DeMar's work is not only important but vital. He has learned from history, and if Americans can apply the principles recalled and set forth herein, then there is hope for a free future.

John W. Whitehead
January 1982
Manassas, Virginia

Preface

If I profess with the loudest voice and clearest exposition every portion of the truth of God except precisely that little point which the world and the devil are at that moment attacking, I am not confessing Christ, however boldly I may be professing Christ.

–Martin Luther

Why another book dealing with the nature of government and politics? Why study government when there are so many great truths in the Bible to expound concerning God, Jesus Christ, salvation, faith, love, and the return of Christ? Are we as Christians getting side-tracked from our proper and central concerns by delving into such "mundane" issues?

Martin Luther (c. 1483-1546) answered these questions when he wrote: "If I profess with the loudest voice and clearest exposition every portion of the truth of God except precisely that little point which the world and the devil are at that moment attacking, I am not confessing Christ, however boldly I may be professing Christ. Where the battle rages, there the loyalty of the soldier is proved and to be steady on all the battlefield besides is mere flight and disgrace if he flinches at that one point."

The battle today is over lordship. The issue of politics today is the issue of sovereignty. Who is the Lord of all of life to whom man must give his total allegiance, Christ or Caesar? The answer to this question is the difference between liberty and slavery, justice and tyranny.

The critical issue of our day is the relationship of Christ and His Word to our political and legal system in the United States. Who has jurisdiction over every aspect of American society, Jesus Christ or the State? Is this to be a Christian nation or a humanistic nation? The only faithful answer that a Bible-believing Christian can give is this: "Blessed is the nation whose God is the LORD" (Psalm 33:12). "For the LORD is our judge, the LORD is our lawgiver, the LORD is our king; He will save us" (Isaiah 33:22).

The Christian's study of the Word of God must bring with it the desire and the ability to make application where Scripture makes application. If Scripture speaks to civil government then civil government must be called upon to acknowledge the Lord of Scripture and be reconstructed according to His demands. A.A. Hodge's words are to the point and just as applicable today as they were a century ago:

> If Christ is really king, exercising original and immediate jurisdiction over the State as really as he does over the church, it follows necessarily that the general denial or neglect of his rightful lordship, any prevalent refusal to obey that Bible which is the open law-book of his kingdom, must be followed by political and social as well as moral and religious ruin. If professing Christians are unfaithful to the authority of their Lord in their capacity as citizens of the State, they cannot expect to be blessed by the indwelling of the Holy Ghost in their capacity as members of the Church. The kingdom of Christ is one, and cannot be divided in life or in death. If the Church languishes, the State cannot be in health; and if the State rebels against its Lord and King, the Church cannot enjoy his favour. If the Holy Ghost is withdrawn from the Church, he is not present in the State; and if he, the only "Lord, the Giver of life," be absent, then all order is impossible, and the elements of society lapse backward to primeval night and chaos...I charge you, citizens of the United States, afloat on your wide sea of politics, THERE IS ANOTHER KING, ONE JESUS: THE SAFETY OF THE STATE CAN BE SECURED ONLY IN THE WAY OF HUMBLE AND WHOLE-SOULED LOYALTY TO HIS PERSON AND OF OBEDIENCE TO HIS LAW (A.A. Hodge, *Evangelical Theology*, pp. 246-248).

The political choice before us is Christ or chaos. Is Jesus "the King of kings and Lord of lords" or is He not? That is the question before American Christians. The issue is anything but peripheral.

Special Features

The *God and Government* textbook series is designed for individual, church, school, seminar, and group Bible study. The question and answer format requires you to pause and to consider the issues under study in the light of biblical revelation before moving to another question. This educational device is necessary for a faithful application of Scripture to all of life. More often than not books are designed for reading, not reflection and meditation. The following special features are included to make the *God and Government* textbook series a true student's handbook:

1. Each lesson begins with an introduction to provide a frame of reference for the questions that follow.

2. The questions are designed to deal with each topic from a number of vantage points. This is why a number of the questions have a substantial list of Bible passages.

3. Scripture passages are included to encourage you to begin your study from a biblical perspective, always asking the question, "What does God's Word say about this issue?" Keep in mind that the interpretation of any one passage must be interpreted in its larger context. Consider the paragraph, chapter, book, author, Testament (Old or New), period of biblical history, audience, circumstances surrounding the writing, and other interpretive factors when formulating your answer.

4. Each lesson ends with a summary designed to focus your attention on each lesson's main theme. I've chosen quotations from respected Christian authors to summarize each chapter.

5. The unique feature of this textbook series is the answers supplied to each of the questions. The answers are comprehensive in most cases. Try to formulate your own answer before turning to the supplied answers.

The Landing of the Pilgrims, 1620. *A great hope and inward zeal they had of laying some good foundation, or at least to make some way thereunto, for propagating and advancing the Gospel of the Kingdom of Christ in those remote parts of the world; yea, though they should be but even as stepping stones unto others for the performing of so great a work.*

6. Volume 1 of *God and Government* seeks to establish the Christian history of the United States prior to the drafting of the Constitution in 1787. Lesson 7 is designed to dispel the myth that the Christian faith was not the central force behind the establishment of America and her institutions. In order to enhance your understanding and appreciation of America's rich Christian history, American Vision has produced *America's Christian History: The Untold Story.* This award-winning audio presentation uses original source documents, sound effects, music, and drama to portray the true story of America's founding.

How to Use this Textbook

You will gain maximum benefit from this textbook by following these suggestions:

1. Pray for wisdom and insight from the Holy Spirit as you study each lesson. You are dealing with the Word of God when you are searching the Scriptures for answers to the questions, thus, only the Spirit of God can bring out a text's true meaning.

2. Read the introduction to each lesson. They are designed to establish the context for the topic being studied.

3. Answer the questions using the Scripture passages as the foundation for your answer. Do not expect to develop as complete an answer as is found in the workbook. You should, however, be able to summarize an answer in the space provided under each question. An extra lined answer sheet is included in the back of this volume for longer answers. This answer sheet can be copied and passed out to students who are using the textbook as a workbook or supplement to a course in government or history.

4. For group study, each student should answer the questions before the group meets for discussion. This will allow more time for evaluation and informed exchange of ideas. A leader who is familiar with the topics presented in this volume should be chosen for each lesson to guide the discussion.

5. Each lesson is designed for a series of forty-five minute to one-hour sessions to be taught over a period of ten to twelve weeks. The study should not go on for a long period of time. It is best for students to want more than for them to say that they have had enough. The aim is to *introduce* Christians to the topics in such a way that they will want to study on their own.

6. Evaluate current events in the light of the biblical principles under discussion. Daily newspapers, magazines, radio and television news programs, talk shows, and issues that arise during local and national elections are helpful sources of information to help you think through the issues as they arise through your study.

7. Based on your study, construct biblical solutions that can replace humanistic policies and programs. Develop strategies to implement these biblical solutions to correct current problems. This might mean establishing additional study groups so these biblical principles can be shared. As more people learn what the solutions are they will be better equipped to implement them. Pray that we do not hear this lament for our nation: "My people are destroyed for lack of knowledge" (Hosea 4:6).

The Bible is the foundation of life. In this Currier print entitled "Reading the Scriptures," the following verse was attached: *Search the Scriptures, for in them ye have eternal life, and they are they which testify of me* (John 5:39).

Joseph Story (1779-1845), Associate Justice of the United States Supreme Court. From *Commentaries on the Constitution of the United States*, sections 1874, 1877.

The real object of the First Amendment was not to countenance, much less to advance, Mahomedanism, or Judaism, or infidelity, by prostrating Christianity; but to exclude all rivalry among Christian sects, and to prevent any national ecclesiastical establishment which should give to a hierarchy the exclusive patronage of the national government. It thus cut off the means of religious persecution (the vice and pest of former ages), and of the subversion of the rights of conscience in matters of religion which had been trampled upon almost from the days of the Apostles to the present age. . . .

Probably at the time of the adoption of the Constitution, and of the first amendment to it . . . the general, if not the universal, sentiment in America was that Christianity ought to receive encouragement from the State, so far as was not incompatible with the previous rights of conscience and the freedom of religious worship. An attempt to level all religions and to make it a matter of state policy to hold all in utter indifference would have created universal disapprobation, if not universal indignation.

—Joseph Story

There is a direct relationship between godly self-government, family government, and the relationships of life. The self-governed individual prospers in all his labors.

Lesson 1

Self-Government
and
Family Government

What is government? When this question is asked, most people respond by equating government solely with a centralized state. Even our language reflects the confusion: "Government? It's in Washington," or "The government will take care of its citizens through its many programs." Both of these statements reflect a misunderstanding of the true nature of government. They portray the idea that the only governing institution is a political one. Historically, however, the term "government" was always qualified in some way, unlike our present-day definitions.

Our educational system reflects the same confusion. A generation ago high school classes dealing with state government were given the title "Civics." The emphasis was on the function of government in civil matters. This is no longer the case. Such classes are now given the broad title of "Government," implying that the many governments are absorbed into one all-encompassing government. Before World War I, textbooks dealing with national government were qualified with the title "Civil." An example of this can be seen in a textbook used in 1903: *Elements of Civil Government*. According to its author, "The family...is a form of government, established for the good of children themselves, and the first government that each of us must obey" (p. 18). The book continues by defining five areas of civil government: "the township or civil district, the village or the city, the county, the State, and the United States" (p. 18). The term "government," as the older educational definition indicates, is broader than the state. Textbook writers were aware that there were personal, family, church, school, and civil governments, each having a legitimate realm of authority. The state was seen as only one government among many.

To deny the validity of the many governments and the responsibilities that each has under God, would be to deny the authority that belongs to each of them in the realm of their activity. If we as individuals neglect our personal governing duties, then we can expect the state to assume the role of all other legitimate governments and claim to be the sole government, while labeling all others as counterfeits. Therefore, to see the state as the only governing institution "is destructive of liberty and of life" (R.J. Rushdoony, *Politics of Guilt and Pity*, p. 332).

The moral principles and precepts contained in the scriptures ought to form the basis of all our civil constitutions and laws. All the miseries and evils which men suffer from vice, crime, ambition, injustice, oppression, slavery, and war, proceed from their despising or neglecting the precepts contained in the Bible.

–Noah Webster

The concept of the multiplicity of governments was as old as our country, because the principles were extracted from biblical principles. Noah Webster's definition of government in his *American Dictionary of the English Language* (1828) reflects the biblical concept of the diversity of governmental authority. Webster defined government in this way: "Direction; regulation. 'These precepts will serve for the *government* of our conduct.' Control; restraint. 'Men are apt to neglect the *government* of their temper and passions.'"

While Noah Webster, in 1828, defined government in terms of personal self-control, most modern definitions largely limit government to the realm of institutions, especially civil or statist governments. This is made evident by the fact that the definition for civil government is placed first in modern dictionaries. Nowhere are self and family governments even listed. For example, *Webster's New World Dictionary* (1972), defines government in this way: "The exercise of authority over a state, district, organization, institution, etc."

Noah Webster, in the older definition, even goes on to include family government as part of the complete definition before he deals with the government of an individual state or nation. He defines family government as: "The exercise of authority by a parent or householder. 'Children are often ruined by a neglect of *government* in parents.'" According to the Bible, it is the duty of parents to govern in the home: "And fathers, do not provoke your children to anger; but bring them up in the discipline and instruction of the Lord" (Ephesians 6:4). It is not the duty of a civil government to interfere with the affairs of the family. Too often, however, parents neglect their God-given duty to raise their children in the "nurture and admonition of the Lord." When this happens, we can expect the state to take an increasingly dominant role in family affairs. Such a role is to the detriment of the family. The state on many occasions has even claimed ownership of children.

If generations continue to be indoctrinated with the modern definition, as they have been, they will neglect their own personal, family, church, and local governing duties. They will believe that these duties are outside their area of authority and responsibility. Each generation will become more dependent on the "benevolent" state for care and security. We are beginning to see such a trend. "Today, most Americans have lost their faith in Christ as Savior, and they expect civil government to be their savior. They have no desire for the responsibilities of self-government, and so they say to politicians, 'Do thou rule over us.' Instead of Jesus Christ as their good shepherd, they elect politicians to be their shepherds on a program of socialistic security for all" (R.J. Rushdoony, *Law and Liberty*, p. 61)

Government, then, in our American Christian heritage which was formulated from biblical principles, begins with the individual and extends outward to include all institutions. Presently, however, most Americans are unaware of the varied nature of government. The civil government has assumed responsibility to be *the* government. It is sad to say that many Americans are thankful that Washington has relieved them from what they believe is the heavy burden of governing themselves, their families, churches, and schools. If the people of the United States do not once again establish self, family, church, local, state, and national governments to their proper places of power and authority, our nation is doomed.

The central focus of all realms of government is the regenerating work of Jesus Christ. Institutions and civil governments are made up of people who are governed by the condition of their hearts. If the heart is in rebellion against God, we can expect undisciplined and ungovernable people. If the heart has been made new in Christ, we can expect a people who will govern their lives according to the governing principles of Scripture. A.A. Hodge speaks of the essence of the new heart, regeneration, as consisting of "the implantation of a new governing principle of life—from the fact that it is a 'new birth' [John 3:3], a 'new creation' [2 Corinthians 5:17], wrought by the mighty power of God in execution of his eternal purpose of salvation, and that it is as necessary for the most moral and amiable as for the morally abandoned" (*A Commentary on the Confession of Faith*, p. 238).

The civil government of the United States is decentralized. We are a single nation made up of a number of sovereign states. The many states created the single nation: *E Pluribus Unum* (out of many, one). The stability of all these governments is dependant upon the self-governed individual under God's government.

Questions for Discussion

Before beginning this section, read "What is Government?" This brief chapter immediately follows Lesson 10. The concepts outlined in the *God and Government* series are summed up in "What is Government?"

Self-Government

1. Compare Noah Webster's definition of *government* in his *An American Dictionary of the English Language* with that of modern dictionaries and contemporary usage of the word *government* in the media (newspapers, magazines, and television). How are they the same? How do they differ?

_____

_____

_____

_____

_____

_____

_____

_____

_____

2. What does the Bible have in mind when it describes God's government in the singular? (Isaiah 9:6-7; Psalm 2; Daniel 4:34-37; 1 Timothy 6:15-16; Revelation 19:6; Ephesians 5:22-34; Hebrews 12:1-13; Romans 13:4; cf. 12:19)

_____

_____

_____

_____

_____

_____

_____

_____

_____

_____

3. What does the Bible mean by self-government or self-control, and what is the foundation of self-government? (Genesis 39:7-23; 41:38-49; 49:4, 23-24; Proverbs 13:24; 16:9; Galatians 5:16-26)

_____

_____

_____

_____

_____

_____

_____

4. How does self-government differ from autonomous government, and in what ways is self-government often denied? (Judges 17:6; Genesis 3:1-14; James 1:13-18; 4:7)

_____

_____

_____

_____

_____

_____

5. What is the relationship between God's _singular_ government and the _many_ institutional governments like family, church, and civil government, and how does the principle of the "many" governments work itself out in family, church, and State? (Ephesians 6:1; Matthew 16:19; 18-15-18; 1 Corinthians 6:1-11; Hebrews 13:17; 1 Peter 2:13-14; 1 Timothy 3:1-8)

_____

_____

_____

_____

_____

_____

_____

Family Government

1. Using the definition of government found in the the self-government and family government sections and the Appendix on "What Is Government?," describe the biblical nature of family government, comparing it with the model government of the Triune God. (**Sovereignty:** Matthew 6:9; Acts 17:25; Matthew 7:9-11; Matthew 4:4; cf. Deuteronomy 8:3; 6:6-9; Psalm 78:1-8; Acts 17:29; John 8:31-47; Romans 7:15; Acts 16:25-34; Ephesians 6:4; Colossians 3:21; 2 Timothy 3:15. **Representation:** 1 Corinthians 11:3; Ephesians 5:22-33; Matthew 3:17; Mark 9:7; Luke 22:42; Galatians 4:6; Romans 8:12-17. **Law:** Hebrews 3:6; Luke 22:42; Ephesians 6:1. **Jurisdiction:** Proverbs 13:24; 22:15; 23:13; 29:15; Hebrews 12:5-6; see vv. 7-11. **Continuity:** Matthew 28:18; Psalm 2:8; Ephesians 6:1-3; 1 Samuel 2:12-17, 22-26; 4:11).

_____

_____

_____

_____

_____

_____

_____

2. What is the origin of family government, and in what ways is the biblical model of family government coming under attack? (Genesis 2:21-25; 4:1-2; Matthew 19:4-6; Ephesians 6:1-2; Deuteronomy 21:18-21; Proverbs 22:6; Ephesians 6:4; Exodus 20:14; Deuteronomy 5:18; Leviticus 18:6-18; 19:29; 21:19; Deuteronomy 23:17; Leviticus 18:22-23; Deuteronomy 23:17; 1 Corinthians 7:2; 1 Timothy 3:2; Leviticus 21:7; Matthew 19:3-9; Mark 10:2-12; Luke 16:8)

_____

_____

_____

_____

_____

_____

_____

3. In what ways is the biblical view of the family being redesigned, and what will be the results? (1 Corinthians 11:1-15; Judges 4; Isaiah 3:12-26; 4:1)

_____

_____

_____

_____

_____

_____

4. How can the biblical family be used to restore the republic? (1 Timothy 5:8; Deuteronomy 21:17; Psalm 78:1-8; Proverbs 13:22; 1 Timothy 3:4-5; Deuteronomy 1:13; cf. Exodus 18:17-26; 1 Samuel 2:12-17, 22-36; 1 Corinthians 6:2; Exodus 20:12; 1 Kings 21)

_____

_____

_____

_____

_____

_____

Summary

"There are few statements today about the opportunity and the obligation of a Christian home in a republic. Yet there is no single element in America which contributes more significantly to the success of Christian Constitutional government. It is in the home where the foundations of Christian character are laid. It is in the home where Christian self-government is learned and practiced. Yet, the Christian American who is aware of the particular challenges to America's Christian character and to the Constitutional form of government still inclines to political education outside the home. Thus, while parents are active politically, educationally, religiously, it becomes necessary for other agencies — the school, the church, the community — to pick up the responsibility for making home the first sphere of government in the republic. Needless to say they cannot substitute what only the home can provide" (Rosalie J. Slater, _Teaching and Learning America's Christian History_, p. 3).

Answers to Questions for Discussion

Self-Government

1. Noah Webster's *An American Dictionary of the English Language* (first published in 1828) defines government this way:

GOVERNMENT, *n.* Direction; regulation. "These precepts will serve for the *government* of our conduct."

2. Control; restraint. "Men are apt to neglect the *government* of their temper and passions."

3. The exercise of authority; direction and restraint exercised over the actions of men in communities, societies or states; the administration of public affairs, according to the established constitution, laws and usages, or by arbitrary edict. "Prussia rose to importance under the *government* of Frederick II."

4. The exercise of authority by a parent or householder. "Children are often ruined by a neglect of *government* in parents." Let family *government* be like that of our heavenly Father, mild, gentle and affectionate." *Kollock.*

Noah Webster states that government begins with the *individual* and the "regulation" of his "conduct." Government, in the older definition, is moral and personal before it is practical and institutional. Without self-governed individuals who follow some moral code, we cannot expect good family, church, and civil governments to be developed. Self-government (or self-control) under God is the foundation of any society.

Self-government undergirds all institutional governments, including parents and children in *family* government, pastors, elders, deacons, and members in *ecclesiastical* (church) government, and civil servants and citizens in *civil* governments at all jurisdictional levels (city, county, state, and national). Noah Webster did not define government solely in *civil* or *political* terms.

11

Many modern dictionaries obscure the fundamental moral and diverse applicational features of government. The term "government" is most often equated with politics than associated with the moral flow of power and force in the operation of family, church, and a decentralized political order. There is little or no mention of family and ecclesiastical governance in modern usage. While there is some discussion of "moral conduct or behavior," the relationship between "moral conduct" and good government is rarely if ever discussed in modern dictionaries.

The Capitol represents the national government, one *civil government* among many other *civil governments*. Our nation's federal civil government was not designed to be *the* government ruling over all lesser governments, although this seems to be the way it is thought of today.

In modern usage "government," especially in the media, has become a synonym for *civil* government alone. "Government" is an all-embracing term that is used for anything done by the State ("State" is being used as a synonym for the highest level of *civil* government: national or federal):

- *The government* releases crime figures
- *The government* sets educational policy
- *The government* delivers unemployment statistics
- *The government* administers tax policy
- *The government* establishes monetary reform

By phrasing these statements in this way, the assumption is that there are no other governing institutions with legitimate jurisdictional authority. A more correct description of the State's function would have some qualifiers attached to the word *government*.

This more biblical understanding of government leads us to consider the following points. First, civil government (the same could be said for family and church governments) is decentralized. We have civil governments at the *national* or *federal* level, fifty *state* governments, dozens of *county* seats, and hundreds of *city* governments. Second, civil government is just one government among many other legitimate non-civil governments. Civil government, therefore, should only have jurisdiction in those areas where it has biblical and constitutional authority to govern. There are governments (e.g., family and church) which also have legitimate jurisdiction in their God-ordained spheres.

2. When the Bible speaks of "government" in the singular, it refers to the comprehensive government of Jesus Christ; a government that encompasses and rules over all individuals, governments, and nations:

> For a child will be born to us, a son will be given to us; and *the government will rest on His shoulders*; and His name will be called Wonderful Counselor, Mighty God, Eternal Father, Prince of Peace. There *will be no end to the increase of His government or of peace*, on the throne of David and over His kingdom, to establish it and to uphold it with justice and righteousness from then on and forevermore. The zeal of the LORD of hosts will accomplish this (Isaiah 9:6-7).

We know that the child spoken of in this passage is Jesus (Luke 2:11). So then, the government of Jesus began at His birth and will never end: "There will be no end to the increase of His government or of peace." He is presently sitting "on the throne of David and over His kingdom." While some see this fulfillment as yet future, Scripture tells us that Jesus (David's son and Lord: Mark 12:35-37), has ascended to the throne that is rightly His (Acts 2:22-36; esp. vv. 30-36; cp. 7:54-56). God fulfilled His promise to David in the resurrection and ascension of Jesus, David's descendant (Matthew 1:1; Romans 1:3; 15:12):

> The LORD has sworn to David, a truth from which He will not turn back; "Of the fruit of your body I will set upon your throne" (Psalm 132:11).

When Jesus was raised from the dead, God "seated Him at His right hand in the heavenly places, far above all rule and authority and power and dominion, and every name that is named, not only in this age, but also in the one to come. And He put all things in subjection under His feet, and gave Him as head over all things to the church" (Ephesians 1:20-23). This is why Jesus is called the "King of kings, and the Lord of lords" (Revelation 19:15).

No human government or institution can claim to be independent of God's government since Jesus is their "Lord" and "King" (Revelation 17:14). Neither can any government claim to be the sole government denying all other governments. In Psalm 2, rulers are to "Worship the LORD with reverence" by doing "homage to the Son, lest He become angry" and they "perish in the way" (2:12). King Nebuchadnezzar acknowledged that God "does according to His will in the host of heaven and among the inhabitants of earth" (Daniel 4:35). This shows that God's government is autonomous, that is, He is a law (*nomos*) unto Himself (*autos*): "He does according to His will." Man and his governments, on the other hand, must "honor the King of heaven, for His works are true and His ways just, and He is able to humble those who walk in pride" (v. 37). This makes the governments of men *dependent* upon the one government of God. Paul describes God as "the *only* Sovereign, the King of kings and Lord of lords" (1 Timothy 6:15). God is the sole Governor ("the only Sovereign") who delegates authority to earthly "kings" and "lords."

3. Self-government is synonymous with self-control. A self-governed individual is someone who can regulate his attitudes and actions without the need for external coercion. Reuben, one of Jacob's twelve sons, is described as a man who "boils over": "Reuben, you are my first-born; my might and the beginning of my strength, preeminent in dignity and preeminent in power. Uncontrolled [Lit., *boiling over*] as water, you shall not have preeminence, because you went up to your father's bed; then you defiled it — he went up to my couch" (Genesis 49:4). Reuben was preeminent in nearly everything, but his lack of self-control took from him the status and privileges of the first-born (a double portion of his father's inheritance). This single text shows us that there is a relationship between self-government and godly leadership. Those who cannot govern themselves cannot govern others (1 Timothy 3:1-8).

On the other hand, Joseph exhibited self-control (self-government) even under great temptation and the possibility of personal gain (Genesis 39:7-23; 49:23-24). He is then blessed beyond any of his brothers, by Pharaoh and Jacob alike. In Egypt he is made a ruler (41:38-49), and through his children, Ephraim and Manasseh, Joseph receives a double portion of the promised land as if he were the firstborn.

God desires self-government to operate in all His creatures. Those who will not rule themselves by God's standard will be ruled by others. *The law is not made for a righteous man, but for those who are lawless and rebellious, for the ungodly and sinners, for the unholy and profane, for those who kill their fathers or mothers, murderers and immoral men and homosexuals and kidnappers and liars and perjurers, and whatever else is contrary to sound teaching* (1 Timothy 1:9-10).

A self-governed individual obeys the law of God *from the heart*, while someone who lacks self-control must be *forced* to obey. Those who are not self-governed need to be controlled by an *external* governor. This is why Scripture tells us "that the law is not made for a righteous man, but for those who are lawless and rebellious, for the ungodly and sinners, for the unholy and profane, for those who kill their fathers or mothers, murderers and immoral men and homosexuals and kidnappers and liars and perjurers, and whatever else is contrary to sound teaching" (1 Timothy 1:9-10). For children, a spanking may be needed for rebellion against parents in family government (Proverbs 13:24).

15

Of course, parents work for the day when their children will learn to govern their behavior without the need of external correction. A student who refuses to do his homework may be forced to stay after school until he completes it. A self-governed student does his homework, considering the consequences if he fails to do it, having learned that self-government brings the reward of freedom after school, the absence of anxiety, good grades, a good relationship with his parents and teachers, and the prospect of future employment.

An ungoverned citizen reverts to crime to satisfy his uncontrolled desires. He might steal, vandalize, murder, or rape. His failure to govern himself means that others must govern him, protecting the larger society from his destructiveness and rebellion.

Self-government is generated through the power of God's Spirit (Galatians 5:16-26), therefore, ultimately we cannot talk about self-government without addressing the person and work of Jesus Christ. Men fail in self-government because they are in rebellion against God. The heart of rebellious sinners, dead in trespasses and sins, must be regenerated. Only the renewing work of the Holy Spirit can affect such a change. For the unbeliever, the law and the threat of punishment keep him in check (1 Timothy 1:9-10). Even for the Christian, because he is still a sinner, the law and the consequences that come with disobedience (punishment) keep him in check as well.

Any society that has a history of self-control among the citizenry has at its foundation a biblical moral order. Those nations that attempt to copy the *fruit* of a Christian society without copying the *root* (the regenerating work of the Holy Spirit) will eventually degenerate and collapse. Christian virtues will be counterfeited, and attempts will be made by the State (civil government at the national level), in a desire for a man-centered utopia, to force a humanistically conceived "morality" in the name of "the people." Such regimes more often than not end in bloodshed.

We should not expect any long-term change in society without a radical change in the belief patterns of the citizenry. This means that a revival and reformation must sweep across America with millions converted. From new hearts will flow a new, although not a perfect, society. Societal change without personal regeneration is a myth and an impossibility. If we are going to see society changed, then we must see individuals changed. Evangelism, therefore, cannot be divorced from our talk about "good government." But these

16

internally transformed individuals need a guidebook to know what needs to be changed and how to do it. The Bible is that guidebook:

> Diffuse the knowledge of the Bible, and the hungry will be fed, and the naked clothed. Diffuse the knowledge of the Bible, and the stranger will be sheltered, the prisoner visited, and the sick ministered unto. Diffuse the knowledge of the Bible, and Temperance will rest upon a surer basis than any mere private pledge or public statute. Diffuse the knowledge of the Bible, and the peace of the world will be secured by more substantial safeguards than either the mutual fear, or the reciprocal interests, of princes or of people. Diffuse the knowledge of the Bible, and the day will be hastened, as it can be hastened in no other way, when every yoke shall be loosened, and every bond broken, and when there shall be no more leading into captivity. . . . (John Winthrop, cited in Verna M. Hall, ed., *The Christian History of the American Revolution*, p. 19).

Family, church, and civil governments reflect the self-government of the people, whether good or bad. At the civil level, a nation gets what it votes for.

John Adams (1735-1826) wrote: *Our Constitution was made only for a moral and religious people. It is wholly inadequate to the government of any other.*

17

Civil government, no matter how righteously conceived, cannot make people better. Leadership, like water, rises to its own level, the righteousness or unrighteousness of the people. George Washington, in his Farewell Address, gave this advice to the nation: "Of all the dispositions and habits which lead to political prosperity, religion and morality are indispensible supports" (September 17, 1796).

No governing document can create freedom, national stability, and security. The best political intentions are no match for the will of the people. Self-governed people who acknowledge the sovereignty of God determine a nation's future. The choice of autonomous rights over God-prescribed responsibilities will mean the decay of a nation. John Adams wrote: "Our Constitution was made only for a moral and religious people. It is wholly inadequate to the government of any other." When self-government is abandoned for self-serving opportunism, we should expect a decline in the health of the nation.

Those who will not exhibit self-control or self-government often find themselves being governed by harsher means. Better to control yourself than to loose your freedoms at the control of others.

4. The word autonomy means self-law, that is, a person makes his or her own laws without any regard for a higher law. A person who claims autonomy is a law unto himself, answerable to no one but himself. When the term *self-government* is used, we do not mean that the individual is an independent authority who can legitimately claim that his own views of morality are lawful. We all must answer to God's law. Only God is ethically autonomous. He is a law unto Himself, and His law is righteous and good because He is righteous and good. His law is a reflection of His character. Since His character cannot change, His law cannot change. "For I, the LORD, do not change; therefore you, O sons of Jacob, are not consumed" (Malachi 3:6). Man's law is a reflection of his character.

Autonomy, the belief that man is capable of establishing a righteous law code independent of the Bible, often leads to family, ecclesiastical, and civil anarchy because these individuals assume that any flaw in a government to which they are responsible to submit gives them the license to rebel: Children rebel against parents in family government (Exodus 21:15, 17; Mark 7:10-13), church members will not submit to those who rule over them in ecclesiastical government (Hebrews 13:17), and citizens rebel against civil rulers in civil government (Acts 5:36-37).

There are times, however, when the governments that are over us must be disobeyed. But even here the Bible sets forth the parameters for non-compliance. Such a stand is an appeal of last resort *to the Bible* under extreme circumstances (e.g., Exodus 1:15-22; Acts 5:29).

The denial of self-government is the denial of personal responsibility. When Adam and Eve were confronted by God because of their sin, they immediately blamed someone else for their faults. Eve blamed the serpent: "The serpent deceived me, and I ate" (Genesis 3:13). Adam blamed Eve, but ultimately he blamed God: "The woman whom *Thou* gavest to be with me, she gave me from the tree, and I ate" (Genesis 3:12; cf. James 1:13-18). Cain, after murdering his brother, evaded the charges by asking, "Am I my brother's keeper?" (Genesis 4:9). The sinner is "tempted when he is carried away and enticed by *his own* lust" (James 1:14). The environment cannot be blamed. Adam and Even sinned under the best of environmental conditions.

Even the devil cannot be blamed when we fall into sin. While he can tempt us, he cannot force us to sin since Christians have the ability to "resist the devil" with the result that he will "flee" from us (James 4:7). Resisting, of course, is not enough. We must replace a negative ("resist") with a positive: "Submit therefore to God" (v. 7). The Apostle Paul would not have instructed us to "flee from youthful lusts" if we did not have the ability to do so (2 Timothy 2:22).

5. The jurisdictionally limited and delegated governments of family, church, and State are but a reflection of God's single government which is in the likeness of His holy character. This is why the individual in self-government is to be holy as God is holy. The love that Jesus expressed in giving His life for the church is to be followed by husbands in their love for their wives in family government (Ephesians 5:22-34). Equally, the discipline that fathers give their children is a model of God's discipline of His children (Hebrews 12:1-13). This is why children are commanded to obey their parents *in the Lord* (Ephesians 6:1). There is real authority here and parents have jurisdiction within their own family government.

The State is God's "minister . . ., an avenger who brings wrath upon the one who practices evil" in the area of civil government (Romans 13:4; cf. 12:19). With these principles in mind, we can better understand why Peter commands us to "submit" ourselves "for the Lord's sake to every human institution, whether to a king as the one in authority, or to governors as sent by him for the punishment of evildoers and the praise of those who do right" (1 Peter 2:13-14).

Church members are part of a jurisdictional government called "ecclesiastical government." The Church is given the "keys of the kingdom of heaven," and with these keys the leadership can "bind" and "loose" within the Church (Matthew 16:19). The Church, that is, those who are in authority in ecclesiastical government, have the authority to excommunicate unrepentant members (Matthew 18:15-18). The Church is even given power to handle legal matters within their jurisdictional sphere that many would see as the exclusive power of the State (1 Corinthians 6:1-11). In the book of Hebrews we are told to "obey our leaders, and submit to them; for they keep watch over your souls, as those who will give an account" (Hebrews 13:17). Ultimately, God will demand an accounting on the last day. The State has the power of the sword as God's avenger this side of judgment day: "It does not bear the sword for nothing" (Romans 13:4).

The following diagram illustrates the relationship between the one independent and unlimited government of God and the many dependent, delegated, and limited governments among men:

GOD
Independent, Autonomous, and Unlimited Governing Authority
(Isaiah 9:6-7)

|

MAN AND HUMAN INSTITUTIONS
Dependent, Delegated, and Limited Governing Authority
(Colossians 1:16-17 and Romans 13:1-4)

|

Bible

|

| Family | Church | Civil |
| (Self-Government) | (Self-Government) | (Self-Government) |

Undergirding the three institutional governments is self-government. There will be no fundamental change in civil government until there are fundamental changes in the individual, family, and church.

Hugo Grotius (1583-1645): *He knows not how to rule a Kingdom, that cannot manage a Province; nor can he wield a Province, that cannot order a City; nor he order a City, that knows not how to regulate a Village; nor he a Family that knows not how to Govern himself; neither can any Govern himself unless his reason be Lord, Will and Appetite her Vassals; nor can Reason rule unless herself be ruled by God, and (wholly) be obedient to Him.*

21

Family Government

1. Family government follows the biblical model of all governments. Parents are the **sovereign** rulers in the family. Authority has been delegated to parents from God, and parents ought to reflect the image of God as "Our Father who art in heaven" (Matthew 6:9). The Triune God is a model for family government. God the Father gives us "life and breath and all things" (Acts 17:25). Parents give good gifts to their children as a reflection of their heavenly Father's good gifts (Matthew 7:9-11).

God is our Father in that His words are our sustenance: "Man shall not live on bread alone, but on every word that proceeds out of the mouth of God" (Matthew 4:4; cf. Deuteronomy 8:3). God wants us to look to Him for spiritual and physical provision. In the same way, parents are to feed their children on the Word of God (Deuteronomy 6:6-9; Psalm 78:1-8).

Finally, God is our Father in that He redeems us. In one sense, God is the Father of all (Acts 17:29). But in a very special way, God is Father only to His adopted children. Jesus called the Pharisees children of their father the devil because they repudiated His redeeming work (John 8:31-47). But those who

Our Father, which art in Heaven, hallowed be thy Name; thy Kingdom come, thy Will be done on Earth, as it is in Heaven. Give us this Day our daily Bread; and forgive us our Trespasses, as we forgive them that trespass against us: And lead us not into Temptation, but deliver us from Evil. Amen

In colonial America, the hornbook was used to teach children language basics.

are "in Christ" are adopted children who can now cry out, "Abba! Father!" (Romans 7:15). Parents "redeem" their children through covenantal baptism (Acts 16:25-34), by not "exasperating" and "provoking" them (Ephesians 6:4; Colossians 3:21), teaching them "from childhood . . . the sacred writings which are able to give [them] wisdom that leads to salvation through faith which is in Christ Jesus" (2 Timothy 3:15), and providing them with godly discipline to "deliver his soul from Sheol" (Proverbs 23:14; cf. Hebrews 12:1-13).

There is also a chain of command whereby the husband **represents** Christ as head over his wife and children (1 Corinthians 11:3; Ephesians 5:22-33), the wife **represents** her husband to the children and the world at large, and children are accountable to both mother and father (Proverbs 1:8). Jesus represented His Father and did all His Father's will (Matthew 3:17; Mark 9:7; Luke 22:42). The Holy Spirit works with the Father and the Son in sealing us as adopted children: "And because you are sons, God has sent forth the Spirit of His Son into our hearts, crying, 'Abba! Father!'" (Galatians 4:6; cf. Romans 8:12-17).

There is family **law** to follow. Jesus did all His Father's will as a "faithful Son over His house" (Hebrews 3:6). Jesus did not shrink from obeying the will of His Father: "Father, if Thou art willing, remove this cup from Me; *yet not My will, but Thine be done*" (Luke 22:42). The Spirit works with the Father and the Son so that as Christians we no longer "walk according to the Flesh" but "according to the Spirit" (Romans 8:4). Walking "according to the Spirit" does not mean walking without the law of God. This would divide God's kingdom, pitting the Spirit over against the Father and the Son (Matthew 12:22-29). Neither is "the law of Christ" different from "the law of God." There is one law: The "law of Christ" (Galatians 6:2), the "law of God," the "commands of God" (1 Corinthians 7:19), and the "law of Moses" (1 Corinthians 9:9) are virtually synonymous.

Children, with Jesus as their example, are to "*obey* their parents in the Lord" (Ephesians 6:1): "And [Jesus] went down with them [Mary and Joseph], and He came to Nazareth; and He continued in subjection to them. . ." (Luke 2:51). Children are to hear their "father's instruction"; they are not to "forsake" their "mother's teaching" (Proverbs 1:8; chapters 4-7).

Parents have **jurisdiction** to mete out certain sanctions, the "rod of correction" being the most severe form of punishment (Proverbs 13:24; 22:15; 23:13; 29:15). Our heavenly Father is again the model: "My son, do not regard lightly the discipline of the Lord, nor faint when you are reproved by Him; for those whom the Lord loves He disciplines, and He scourges every son whom He receives" (Hebrews 12:5-6; see vv. 7-11).

Children, obey your parents in the Lord, for this is right. Honor your father and mother (which is the first commandment with a promise), "that it may be well with you, and that you may live long on the earth" (Ephesians 6:1-3).

Obedience brings life (**continuity** and inheritance) while disobedience brings death (discontinuity and disinheritance). Jesus, as the faithful Son, was given "all authority . . . in heaven and on earth" (Matthew 28:18). Why did Jesus receive such an inheritance? Faithfulness. "Ask of Me, and I will surely give the nations as Thine inheritance, and the very ends of the earth as Thy possession" (Psalm 2:8). In the same way, children gain an inheritance through faithfulness: "Honor your father and mother (which is the first commandment with a promise), 'that it may be well with you, *and that you may live long on the earth*'" (Ephesians 6:1-3).

No one can find any happiness in disloyalty to his parents. Esau's marriages to Hittite women were so completely against the advice and entreaties of his parents that Rebecca tells Isaac: "I am weary of my life because of the daughters of Heth" (Gen. 27:46); and Esau drops out of history, leaving no contribution to the affairs of men. Samson is attracted to a Philistine woman. His parents object [Judges 14:1-3], but he obstinately insists, and his protest against their authority submerges him in a deep sea of matrimonial woe (Walter A. Maier, *For Better, Not for Worse*, pp. 315-16).

Long life and the establishment of a family legacy, generally speaking, will not come to those who dishonor their parents (e.g., 1 Samuel 2:12-17, 22-26; 4:11).

2. The family has all the characteristics of a government and mirrors church and civil governments: Rulers (parents/elders/magistrates), subjects (children/members/citizens), law (rules/ordinances/legislation), discipline (correction/restoration/punishment), and inheritance (legacy/reconciliation/peace). In fact, family government is our first government. Before there was a church, family government was established (Genesis 2:21-25). Before there was a State, the family existed (Genesis 4:1-2). In one sense, both ecclesiastical and civil governments are modeled after the family.

> We are . . . led to infer from [biblical history], that the origin of [civil] government arose from paternal government, and is nearly coeval with the creation.
> The duties of rulers and of parents are in many respects nearly allied; both are bound by the holiest ties to promote the happiness of those committed to their charge — both are entitled to respect and obedience; and the most enviable and exalted title any ruler can acquire is "the father of his country" (Joseph Barlett Burleigh, *The American Manual*, pp. 33-34).

God originated the family. It is His design. To attack the biblical family is to attack God and a godly moral order. "The nuclear family is the central building block of Western civilization" ("A New Kind of Spouse in the House," *U. S. News & World Report*, August 21, 1989, p. 14). The husband-wife relationship (Genesis 2:24; Matthew 19:4-6), children under the authority of parents (Ephesians 6:1-2), parents obligated to educate their children (Deuteronomy 21:18-21; Proverbs 22:6; Ephesians 6:4), and the abolition of all deviations in family life are set forth in Scripture: adultery (Exodus 20:14; Deuteronomy 5:18), incest (Leviticus 18:6-18), prostitution (Leviticus 19:29; 21:19; Deuteronomy 23:17), sodomy (Leviticus 18:22-23; Deuteronomy 23:17), polygamy (1 Corinthians 7:2; 1 Timothy 3:2), and divorce (Leviticus 21:7; Matthew 19:3-9; Mark 10:2-12; Luke 16:8).

The biblical family unit has come under attack by a number of radical ideologies. There are, what Alvin Toffler calls, "a bewildering array of family forms: homosexual marriages, communes, groups of elderly people banding together to share expenses (and sometimes sex), tribal grouping among certain ethnic minorities, and many other forms coexist as never before" (Alvin Toffler, *The Third Wave*, p. 212). Existing "family" arrangements are being turned into public policy, with a new definition of the family being implemented into law.

It is part of a trend toward giving homosexual and unmarried couples perks once reserved for men and women with marriage licenses. A half-dozen cities have new laws recognizing some rights for the unmarried. Policy makers "are adopting a concept of family more in line with the way people actually live," says Prof. Arthur Leonard of New York Law School.

The strongest such law is San Francisco's, which lets those who "share one another's lives in an intimate and committed relationship" file a declaration making them eligible for full benefits given to married spouses ("A New Kind of Spouse in the House," *U.S News & World Report*, August 21, 1989, p. 13).

In effect, this means that homosexual relationships are considered legitimate and should be acknowledged and treated as "families."

Feminists have decried the concept of the family, asserting that "the traditional family represents a dysfunctional family unit." Their views assume a belief in evolution where the stronger male-dominated society subjugated women through force and intimidation. For the feminists, the Bible is a "patriarchal document" that should be modernized to fit rapidly changing social mores.

Marxists have lead the way in attempts to abolish the biblical family by asserting that the prohibition against adultery and the command for children to honor their parents is rooted in the concept of private property: Husbands are said to "own" their wives and children like they would own cattle.

> Although communists in Russia have had to retreat from the effort to destroy the family, they are endeavoring through their educational system, including the nurseries, to build loyalty to the Party rather than to the home (James D. Bales, *Communism: Its Faith and Fallacies*, p. 199).

The biblical model of the family is being attacked by liberal theologians as well. This has led them to advocate abortion on demand, homosexuality, lesbianism, pre-marital sex, and adultery.

The godly family is a threat to oppressive civil governments because it does not depend on the State for sustenance and assistance. The biblical family is a legitimate government with rulers (husband and wife) and subjects (children) that supplies what the State can only counterfeit.

3. The redesign of the family begins with the abolition of the biblical concept of headship. Many states have legislated against the husband as the "head of household." Many special interest groups want to make children equal authorities with their parents through a child's "bill of rights." This effectually makes the State the real family where children are to be nurtured and educated. If parents are found to be "unfit" (a condition solely defined by the State), social workers can remove children and make them wards of the State.

With the collapse of the family or the denial of the family's authority, a nation rapidly moves into social anarchy. God, as the source of the family's authority, has located immediate authority in the father or husband (1 Corinthians 11:1-15). When the father abdicates, or certain "interest groups" deny his authority, social rebellion, as described in Isaiah 3:12 results. Women become rulers and children are looked upon as authority equals with the same rights and privileges as their parents. Parents are oppressed in such a view of authority. A crisis in leadership forms (cf. Judges 4). The result is social collapse and captivity (Isaiah 3:16-26). For women, it is a time of "reproach" or "disgrace" (Isaiah 4:1).

4. The family can be instrumental in restoring our nation in numerous ways. The family can care for its own members: "But if anyone does not provide for his won, and especially for those of his own household, he has denied the faith, and is worse than an unbeliever" (1 Timothy 5:8). Rita Kramer writes, "We have asked institutions — the government, the schools — to undertake to direct human nature. The paradox is that as our aims have become increasingly humanitarian, our means have become increasingly controlling" (Rita Kramer, *In Defense of the Family*, p. 19).

When we control our own families, we assume responsibility for family affairs. Families should be setting the agenda for family government. This should not be left to impersonal and distant bureaucrats. Too many families willingly sacrifice their children to such statist institutions as the public schools, day care centers, and welfare agencies. Too many women have adopted the feminist and unbiblical notion of careerism over homemaking to the detriment of the family.

Parents should prepare for the time when they may be unable to work. This will mean saving for the future. Government programs for retirement should not be considered. Financial hardships should be shared by all family members.

For this reason, the first-born son is entitled to a double portion of the family's estate (Deuteronomy 21:17). He has the responsibility of caring for his incapacitated parents. In our day the State has become the "eldest son." In some nations estate taxes consume entire estates. Families are forced to sell off lands and family heirlooms in order to pay estate taxes. The State has asserted its position as the pseudo-family, and now it demands payment for its services.

Education is a function of the family, thus, the family must provide basic Christian teaching rather than turning all education over to the church or the school. The school and church should supplement family education, not replace or overrule it.

The family, therefore, should be future-oriented. We should make decisions with our "children's children" in mind (Psalm 78:1-8). The good and faithful man, through the diligence and dedicated stewardship, leaves an inheritance to his children's children (Proverbs 13:22).

The family must be the child's first school. The family must provide basic Christian teaching rather than turning all education over to the church or school. This means daily instruction in the Bible, prayer, and worship. School and church should supplement these family activities, not replace them. Parents must be overseers of their children's education. Gary North writes:

> Education is the moral responsibility of parents. They are the ones who must determine whether or not their children are being taught the truth. They are responsible before God for the rearing of their children. They are held responsible even for the content of their children's education. This is why it is a great responsibility to bring children into the world (*Unconditional Surrender*, p. 94).

Parents must start schools or school their children at home and thereby take *direct* action for their children's education. This means paying for the services directly. Where parents are dissatisfied with the quality of education presently received, they can demonstrate their displeasure by enrolling their children elsewhere.

The family should provide a training ground for future leadership. Church leadership is cultivated in the family. The church leader "must be one who manages his own household well, keeping his children under control with all dignity (but if a man does not know how to manage his own household, how will he take care of the church of God?)" (1 Timothy 3:4-5). Civil leadership also develops out of family leadership. The choice of rulers in Israel was based on prior leadership in the family and tribe: "Choose wise and discerning and experienced men from your tribes..." (Deuteronomy 1:13; cf. Exodus 18:17-26; 1 Samuel 2:12-17, 22-36). Paul gives us a hint of the extension of godly leadership into the world: "Do you not know that the saints will judge the world?" (1 Corinthians 6:2).

The family is closely tied to private property (Exodus 20:12), and the abolition of private property requires the destruction of the family (1 Kings 21).

Private property is attached to the biblical mandate of dominion. The property tax is one way of dispossessing families of their property. Property values can escalate while income remains constant. This happens in times of government-induced inflation policies. Christians should vote against property tax hikes and work toward tax reduction in all areas.

The family is a government that can provide godly leadership to the world. This leadership has a direct bearing on the future of a community and the nation. In our day, the State has become our "family" assuming responsibility (because families often abdicate) for all the affairs of life, promising security from the womb to the tomb. With such a system productivity and freedom are lost. Property becomes the possession of the State through oppressive taxation and zoning restrictions. A return to the biblical family model brings life to a nation.

A public declaration of humanism in the building of the Tower of Babel. Collective humanity attempting to govern without G

Lesson 2

Ecclesiastical Government and Civil Government

The Bible is opposed to centralism, whether it be political (United Nations) or religious (World Council of Churches). The tower of Babel and God's scattering of those who were involved in its design were judged because of the potential corruption that is inherent in religious and political centralism. "The tower of Babel (Genesis 11) was [a] representative pagan architectural structure. It was probably something like the Babylonian ziggurat, a tower made up of concentric circles which resembled a ladder to heaven from whatever direction an observer approached. Here is the theology that Satan offered to Adam: autonomous man's way to heaven. The tower was a link between heaven and earth, but one which men built, not God. The pinnacle of the tower represented the seat of power, the link between evolving man and the gods" (Gary North, *Unconditional Surrender*, p. 143).

The symbolic purpose of the tower was an attempt by fallen man to unify all creation under a centralized governmental and religious system. "Let's make a name for ourselves" (Genesis 11:4) was "the first public declaration of humanism" (Francis Schaeffer, *Genesis in Space and Time*, p. 152). Corruption and tyranny would be centralized, along with power and authority. This was the danger.

Fallen men believe that they can overthrow the purposes of God through a united display of power as their efforts with the tower of Babel demonstrate. There are other examples as well. Satan tried to secure a host of angels in order to damage God's eternal order. He was soon displaced from his station of honor for his efforts: "And the great dragon was thrown down, the serpent of old who

33

is called the devil and Satan, who deceives the whole world; he was thrown down to the earth, and his angels were thrown down with him" (Revelation 12:9); and his final destruction was sealed: "And the devil who deceived them was thrown into the lake of fire and brimstone, where the beast and the false prophet are also; and they will be tormented day and night forever and ever" (Revelation 20:10).

In the State, as the empire of law, the suffering visited upon transgression is predominately penal. *The sword in the hand of the magistrate is to punish. It smites in the interest of justice. . . . The province of the Church and of the Family is entirely different. Here the object is not punishment, but correction.*

— Benjamin M. Palmer

Satan attempts to marshall the forces of nations against the purposes of God, but to no avail: "Why do the nations rage and the peoples plot in vain? The kings of the earth take their stand and the rulers gather together against the LORD and against His Anointed" (Psalm 2:1-2). All those who seek to centralize power and authority do so in opposition to God. God's response to their efforts show how foolish their attempts are: "He who sits in the heavens laughs, the LORD scoffs at them" (v. 4).

The Bible stresses local government in both Church and State. Paul's letters indicate that there were many churches in Asia Minor, Macedonia, and Achia: Colossae, Ephesus, Philippi, Thessalonica, Corinth, and Galatia. The Apostle John lists churches not mentioned by Paul and other New Testament writers (Revelation 2-3). Of course, there was a very influencial church in Jerusalem (Acts 11:22; 15:1-35). All of these churches had their own ecclesiastical government with their own rulers. But these rulers were not autonomous. They, as well as the membership, are ultimately responsible to Jesus Christ who is "the head of the Church" (Ephesians 5:23).

Churches are mini-republics which find their governing principles from the "church in the wilderness" (Acts 7:38). Church government is neither a pure democracy nor a monarchy (cf. Exodus 18). While the people participate in electing officers, the officers, once they assume a position of leadership, are the rulers who should be obeyed and honored: "Obey your leaders, and submit to them; for they keep watch over your souls, as those who will give an account" (Hebrews 13:17a). But their leadership should not be used as an opportunity to be autocratic or tyrannous: "Let them do this with joy and not with grief, for this would be unproftitable for you" (v. 17b). Again, Jesus is their example.

Elders are to "shepherd the church of God" (Acts 20:28). But the church cannot be effectively shephered from a distance. This is why Paul instructed Titus to "appoint elders in *every city*" (Titus 1:5). Each church was to have a Bible-based ecclesiastical government ruled and shepherded by qualified leaders (1 Timothy 3:1-15). When disputes arose among the churches, *representatives* from the local churches spread abroad came to Jerusalem to settle certain doctrinal matters (Acts 15:1-35).

Civil government is to follow a similar pattern. The affairs of State can best be handled at the local level where the needs of the people and the community are known and the consolidation of power is minimal. The United States civil system of government exhibits a decentralized social order, although attempts at centralization are on the rise.

A meeting of the Westminster Assembly, a group of distinguished European church leaders responsible for the *Westminster Confession of Faith* (1647).

Questions for Discussion

Church Government

"The church is a government and an important one, not only in its exercise of discipline but in its religious and moral influence on the minds of men. Even men outside the church are extensively governed in each era, even if only in a negative sense, by the stand of the church. The failure of the church to provide biblical government has deadly repercussions on a culture" (R.J. Rushdoony, *Politics of Guilt and Pity*, p. 331).

1. Who is qualified to govern in the Church? What are the qualifications for those who are to govern in the Church? (1 Timothy 3:1-7)

_____

_____

_____

_____

2. From whom did the Church receive its governing authority? What is the role of Church government in settling disputes that arise among its members? (Matthew 16:18-19; 18:15-20)

_____

_____

_____

_____

3. What is the extent of the Church's authority in the lives of its members? Why is the authority given? (Matthew 18:15-18; 1 Corinthians 5:1-2, 13; Titus 1:10-16; 1 Timothy 1:18-20)

_____

_____

_____

_____

4. What other governing function does the Church perform with respect to disputes among members? How would this affect civil government? (1 Corinthians 6:1-11)

_____

_____

_____

_____

_____

5. Does the Church, through the leadership of the elders and deacons, perform a governing function for the economic welfare of its members? If so, what is the extent of the Church's governing function in this area? (Acts 6:1-6; 1 Timothy 5:4, 8-10; 2 Corinthians 8:1-15)

_____

_____

_____

_____

_____

6. How does the Church finance its governing responsibilities? Explain. (Matthew 22:21; 1 Corinthians 16:1-4; 2 Corinthians 9:6-15; Proverbs 3:9-10; 19:17; 28:27; Malachi 3:10)

_____

_____

_____

_____

_____

Local Government Versus Centralism

"Civil law is also county law to a great degree, enforced by local courts and by locally elected officials. The American citizen is thus for the most part under county government rather than state and federal government. His basic instruments of civil government are local, residing in the county, and the county is his

37

historic line of defense against the encroachments of state and federal government. In early America, town and county elections were properly regarded as more important than state and federal elections, and property qualifications more strict on the local level" (R.J. Rushdoony, *The Nature of the American System*, p. 10).

1. What purpose did the leaders of the nations have for building the Tower of Babel? What dangers were inherent in their purpose? (Genesis 10:31–11:4)

_____

_____

_____

_____

_____

2. What was God's evaluation of this central governing plan? (Genesis 11:5-9)

_____

_____

_____

_____

3. What was God's purpose in scattering these people? (Genesis 11:8-9)

_____

_____

_____

_____

4. What is the future of the Babel (centralized government) concept? (Daniel 1:1; 2:31-45; 4:11-37; Revelation 16:19; 18:2, 10, 21)

_____

_____

_____

_____

_____

_____

_____

5. How did God structure the nation of Israel so that it would avoid the dangers of centralism? (Deuteronomy 16:18; Joshua 13:7-33)

_____

_____

_____

_____

_____

6. How is local government presented in Israel? (Numbers 11:16; Deuteronomy 16:18; 19:12; 21:2; 22:15; Joshua 4:4; Judges 8:14; Ruth 4:2-4; Proverbs 31:23)

_____

_____

_____

_____

_____

7. How is the concept of local government further expressed and emphasized? (Proverbs 11:14; 24:6; Exodus 18:21-22)

_____

_____

_____

_____

8. How would this system of decentralization work today? (Exodus 18:21-22)

_____

_____

_____

_____

_____

9. How does the New Testament summarize the concept of decentralization? (Romans 13:1, 3, 6, 7)

_____

_____

_____

_____

10. In what ways do you see centralism espoused and localism denied in your own local, county, and state governments?

_____

_____

_____

_____

_____

_____

_____

Summary

"The word government meant, _first_ of all, the self-government of the Christian man, the basic government in all history. _Second_, and very closely and almost inseparably linked with this, government meant the family. Every family is a government; it is man's first church and first school, and also his first state. The government of the family by God's appointed head, the man, is basic to society. _Third_, the church is a government, with laws and discipline. _Fourth_, the school is an important government in the life of a child [and is an extension of family government]. _Fifth_, business or vocations are an important area of government. Our work clearly governs us and we govern our work. _Sixth_, private associations, friendships, organizations, and the like act as a government over us, in that we submit to these social standards and we govern others by our social expectations. _Seventh_, the state is a form of government, and, originally, it was always called _civil_ government in distinction from all these other forms of government.

"But, tragically, today when we say _government_ we mean the state, the federal government, or some other form of civil government. And, more tragically, civil government today claims to be _the_ government over man, not one government among many, but one over-all government. Civil government claims jurisdiction over our private associations, our work or business, our schools and churches, our families, and ourselves. The word government no longer means self-government primarily and essentially; it means the state" (Rousas J. Rushdoony, _Law and Liberty_, p. 59).

Answers to Questions for Discussion

Church Government

1. Only the man who has proved himself in the area of self-government and family government is qualified to govern the Church. "[T]here is a concern for *spiritual qualifications*. The apostles did not ask the believers to consider whether those elected to this office had private wealth so that they could minister out of their own pockets should the church's funds run out. They did not ask whether they were in positions of secular power or influence. Such concerns did not enter in at all. They were simply asked to pick out men who were of good repute, and full of the Spirit and of wisdom" (James Montgomery Boice, *God and History*, p. 152).

2. The Church of Jesus Christ has governing authority because it was instituted by Him. ("For where two or three have gathered in My name, there I am in their midst" [Matthew 18:20].) Jesus states that it is His Church: "Upon this rock I will build My church" (Matthew 16:18). The Church derives its authority from Him to act on His behalf: "I will give you the keys of the kingdom of heaven; and whatever you shall bind on earth shall have been bound in heaven, and whatever you shall loose on earth shall have been loosed in heaven" (16:19). When a dispute arises, which cannot be settled by two individuals or through the counsel of others, it is the duty of the Church, ruled by self-governed elders, to render a decision in Christ's name (see Matthew 18:15-20).

3. The extent of the Church's authority is no greater than what the Bible states. The duty of Church leaders is to keep the Church pure from sinful behavior (1 Corinthians 5:1-2; 6:1-11) and doctrinal error (1 Timothy 4:6, 11; 6:3-5) and to make the offender realize his need of repentance (Matthew 18:15). Those who are called upon to enforce such discipline must always be aware of their responsibility to restore the guilty party if and when he truly repents (2 Corinthians 2:5-11). If repentance is not forthcoming then the offender must be removed from the Church's midst (1 Corinthians 5:2). The elders of the Church have the authority to excommunicate unrepentant sinners from the Church as a doctor would cut a festering growth from a healthy body.

41

Delegates at the Synod of Dort meeting in Dort, Holland, 1619.

4. Disputes among members are to be dealt with by the leadership of the Church. Since Christians are under the authority of the elders, who represent Jesus Christ, and the elders are students of the word of God (cf. 1 Timothy 3:2—"able to teach"), it is natural for the Church to handle disputes among members. Those disputes that did not require the use of physical punishment (the jurisdiction of the state), but were only a matter of judgment between two opinions, could be handled by the Church (1 Corinthians 6:1-11). If disputes among Christians could be settled by Church courts, the cost of civil courts and the backlog of cases could be reduced.

5. Yes, the Church of Jesus Christ is to be a voluntary welfare operation to care for the needs of its members. The Spirit of Christ moved the people of the early Church to sell some of their land holdings in order to meet the temporary needs of the new Christians (Acts 2:43-47). [Notice that this was not the result of "government" action.] When families are not able to care for themselves, the Church, through the generosity of its members, is responsible for meeting their needs. The civil government is to be a protector, not a provider.

6. The Church finances its governing responsibilities through the tithe. Jesus makes it clear that we are to render "to God the things that are God's" (Matthew 22:21). Paul admonishes the Corinthians that God requires His people to return a portion of their income, so that the needs of the Church can be met. Paul admonishes the Corinthians to set aside the collection for the saints "on the first day of every week" (1 Corinthians 16:1-2). These tithes and offerings were used for helping the saints for any needs that they might have (e.g., 1 Timothy 5:9-12). God has seen fit "to demand a tithe for the financing of the Church. In those times of history when the tithe is given properly and the Church does her work with integrity, the state will greatly shrink in size and will require only a minimum in taxation. On the other hand, in those seasons of history, like our own, when the people refuse to tithe, and the Church is not faithfully proclaiming and educating in the Word of God, then the state will grow to massive size, and will exact a terrible tribute. The reformation of the state, then, awaits the reformation of the Church and the proper use of the tithe" (James B. Jordan, "The Mosaic Head Tax and State Financing," *Biblical Economics Today*, Vol. IV, No. 3 [1981]). "Without the tithe, the need for social financing remains, and thus the state tax takes over, as well as statist corruption and misappropriation. A limited state without the tithe is an impossibility, and political conservatives who dream of such an order are fools and dreamers, as are anarchists who dream of existing with no state at all. A strong familistic society and a tithing society can create a wide variety of institutions, schools, and agencies which can take over the basic function of church, school, health, and welfare and thereby shrink the state to its proper dimensions. Social financing is necessary: either the people of God undertake it, or the state will" (R. J. Rushdoony, "Subversion and the Tithe," in *Institutes of Biblical Law*, p. 847f.).

Local Government Versus Centralism

1. The purpose of the Babel project was to bring families and nations together under one power center: "And they said, 'Come, let us build for ourselves a city, and a tower whose top will reach into heaven, and let us make for ourselves a name'" (Genesis 11:4). It is important to realize that there was a diversity of governments which involved themselves in the project: family units, distinct governing regions, and actual nations (a total of seventy). The purpose of the symbolic tower was an attempt to unify all mankind under one central governmental system. "The great tower would dominate the city, both architecturally and culturally. It would serve as the focal point of the political and religious life of the population, and would be a symbol of their unity and strength" (Henry M. Morris, *The Genesis Record*, p. 269). Power and authority would be centralized, along with corruption and tyranny. This form of government would necessitate a central planning system that would obstruct the freedoms of individuals for the supposed benefit of the masses.

Come, let us make bricks and burn them thoroughly...Come, let us build for ourselves a city, and a tower whose top will reach into heaven, and let us make for ourselves a name; lest we be scattered abroad over the face of the whole earth (Genesis 11:3-4).

44

"Throughout Scripture, right up to the book of Revelation, the concept of Babylon stands crucial, Babylon saying, 'We are the gate of God,' and the Bible answering, 'No, this is the place where the basic confusion of language occurred. You are confusion'" (Francis Schaeffer, *Genesis in Space and Time*, p. 153).

2. God's evaluation of this new work was swift and sure. He scattered the people in order to restrain the outworking of their evil imaginations (Genesis 11:6). The consolidation of power and authority had to be broken up for the benefit of mankind (compare pre-flood conditions, Genesis 6:1-8). "Why do the nations rage and the peoples plot in vain? The kings of the earth take their stand and the rulers gather together against the LORD and against His Anointed One" (Psalm 2:1-2). "In a sinful race left to its own devices, one monolithic world state might conceivably put an end to all further political experiment and result in an irreversible totalitarianism" (Alva J. McLain, *The Greatness of the Kingdom*, p. 48).

3. The good result that benefited mankind because of their scattering by God was that each family and tribal unit migrated away from Babel and developed distinctive cultures. The rise of these separate and distinct cultures immediately lessened the power base that a central government would bring. This cultural diversification allowed the relatively independent "states" to govern themselves without the threat of central planning. "As always, there was an element of grace in God's judgment...He...gave to men the conditions externally suitable for political freedom. Localism, the criterion of a decentralized free order, could then be infused with the other requirement of a free society, biblical faith" (Gary North, "The World Trade Incentive," *Chalcedon Report*, No. 102 [February, 1974]).

4. The future of any centralization in opposition to God's moral order is doomed to judgment. Nebuchadnezzar, the king of Babylon, saw himself (represented by a "golden image" [Daniel 3:1] and a mighty tree which "was visible to the end of the earth" [4:20-22]) as the single power in opposition to the God of heaven who gave him the kingdom, the power, the strength, and the glory (Daniel 2:37). "Babylon is a fitting symbol, having its roots in the old dream of Nimrod, of Cain, and of Babel, representing a counterfeit paradise, and an attempt to establish a one-world order without God" (R.J. Rushdoony, *Thy Kingdom Come*, p. 195). Belshazzar and the kingdom of Babylon were

destroyed by the rising Medo-Persian empire (Daniel 5). The stone "cut without hands," representing the kingdom of God, crushes all worldly kingdoms that set themselves up in opposition to Jesus Christ: "And in the days of those kings the God of heaven will set up a kingdom which will never be destroyed,...it will crush and put an end to all these kingdoms, but it will itself endure forever" (Daniel 2:44).

5. God structured the nation of Israel (formerly the land of Canaan) by dividing the land among the twelve tribes. No one tribe could dominate the entire nation because of the influence of the other eleven tribes. Their influence would tend to dilute the power of any one tribe (cf. Joshua 22:10-34). Even though there was not a political centralism in Israel, there was a covenantal centralism: the word of God. "Each of the Israelitish tribes formed a separate state, having a local legislature and a distinct administration of justice. The power of the several states was sovereign within the limits of their reserved rights. Still, there was both a real and a vigorous general government. The nation might have been styled the united tribes, provinces, or states of Israel" (E.C. Wines, *The Hebrew Republic*, p. 98). Even though the United States is not to be identified as the "New Israel," it is important to note that the structure of the first union (the thirteen colonies) was similar in principle to the twelve tribes of Israel—the limitation of a centralized power. This was the intent of the United States Constitution as we shall see in Lesson Eight. During the period of the judges there was an attempt by Abimelech to centralize Israel under his rule (Judges 9:1-6). His reasoning was that centralized rule by one man was preferable to decentralized rule by seventy men. Abimelech's plans were met with a just end (Judges 9:52-57).

6. Local governments were designated as "towns." Every town (literally, "gate") had its own court system with its own rulers and administrators. Affairs of the towns were to be handled by the officials of the town selected "out of all the people" from the town (Deuteronomy 16:18). Local affairs were to be handled by the "elders of the city" because those who ruled are known by the people: "Her husband is known in the gates, when he sits among the elders of the land" (Proverbs 31:23). "Elders formed the basis of civil government. Since men who governed in so extensive a way their own households were best trained to govern, Moses turned to the elders, at the command of God, to form a group of

46

seventy to rule Israel (Num. 11:16). These men governed under Moses and aided him in instructing the people in the implications of the law (Deut. 27:1). Local government was in the hands of elders (Deut. 19:12; 21:2; 22:15; 25:7; Josh. [4:4]; Judges 8:14; Ruth 4:2). These elders are also referred to in the Gospels (Matt. 16:21; 26:47; Luke 7:3)" (R.J. Rushdoony, *Institutes of Biblical Law*, p. 740).

7. The Bible makes it clear that since the authority to rule should not center on one man, we should not expect the ability to rule (wisdom) to reside in one man. "Where there is no guidance, the people fall, but in abundance of counselors (wise men) there is victory" [literally, "deliverance"]. Moreover, since man is a finite creature he is limited in his ability to rule over many. The proof of this is in Exodus 18:21-22. God's people were to organize in groups of ten families with a leader over each group of ten. This civil leader would render judgments when controversies arose within the group. If a controversy broke out between his group of ten families and some other group, the leaders of each group would get together, and the two leaders would render judgment. If the judgment was contested it was appealed to a leader who ruled over a group of fifty. Further appeals could be made. Rule, then, begins at the local or neighborhood level.

8. "You shall select out of all the people [popular elections] able men who fear God [a primary consideration], men of truth, those who hate dishonest gain [it is the duty of citizens to know those being elected]; and you shall place these over them [the people], as leaders of thousands [national], of hundreds [state], of fifties [county], and of tens [precinct]." The numbers are not to be taken as absolutes. Rather, the principle of decentralization is being emphasized. If self, family, and Church governments are operating, the necessity for local government is lessened.

9. Paul, aware of the Old Testament concept of the multiplicity of rulers, summarizes the concept of decentralization when he speaks of "governing authorities" (Romans 13:1), "rulers" (vs. 3), "servants" (vs. 6). Also, he commands us to "render to all what is due them" (vs. 7). The emphasis is on the plurality of powers. The New Testament concept of civil government is consistent with the Old Testament concept of a decentralized state.

Fundamental biblical principles operated in the colonies and were incorporated into the state constitutions. On basic principle was a decentralized civil government. This memorial of our nation's constitutional beginnin expresses well the character of the Union of states.

Lesson 3

The Origin and Development of Civil Government

The study of the origin and development of civil government must begin with the study of God and His position as the Governor of all creation. In the biblical view, the world is wholly the creation of the eternal God. Creation owes its existence to Him: "For from Him and through Him and to Him are all things" (Romans 11:36). The creation is also sustained and governed by Him. Certain facts follow from these first principles that are basic to a Christian view of civil government. The details of the way families function, the management of the created order, the rise and fall of nations, of the powers that be, and of man's relation to all civil powers can only be understood in terms of God as the Supreme Governor of all things.

The Lord God is the universal Governor of all individuals and nations because of His position as Creator of all things: "The Most High God is ruler over the realm of mankind, and He sets over it whomever He wishes" (Daniel 5:21; Isaiah 9:6-7; 1 Corinthians 15:25). Although God's sovereign position is not generally acknowledged in our day, this fundamental truth gave undergirding to our nation's beginnings. John Calvin, the great 16th century reformer, had this to say about the benevolent sovereignty of God's government: "He surely shows himself the protector and vindicator of innocence, while he prospers the life of good men with his blessing, relieves their need, soothes and mitigates their pain, and alleviates their calamities; and in all these things he provides for their salvation" (John T. McNeill, ed., *Institutes of the Christian Religion*, p. 60).

God is not only the Creator of all things, but He is also the sustainer of all

49

He surely shows himself the protector and vindicator of innocence, while he prospers the life of good men with his blessing, relieves their need, soothes and mitigates their pain, and alleviates their calamities; and in all these things he provides for their salvation.

–John Calvin

things: "And He [Jesus] is before all things, and in Him all things hold together" (Colossians 1:17). "That God sustains the world of created things is the theological doctrine of preservation. That He governs it is the doctrine of providence. The Bible specifically rejects the notion that God in creation placed the creation under such full control of laws and secondary causes that it operates completely without Him [deism]. Rather, though God ceased from His works of creation (Gen 2:3, cf. Heb 4:10), His power continues to go forth uninterruptedly to keep it in existence and operation (Neh 9:6; Ps 36:6; 104; Ac 17:28; Col 1:17; Heb 1:1-2)" (Robert Duncan Culver, *Toward a Biblical View of Civil Government*, pp. 42-43).

Moreover, there are no independent governments, whether they be individual, family, school, Church, or national. Every individual, institution, or nation is responsible to other individuals, institutions, and nations. All are ultimately responsible to God. God rules wives through husbands in marriage government: "Wives, be subject to your own husbands, as to the Lord..." (Ephesians 5:22f); children through their parents in family governments: "Children, obey your parents in the Lord, for this is right. Honor your father and mother (which is the first commandment with a promise), that it may be well with you, and that you may live long on the earth" (Ephesians 6:1-3).

Students are to obey their teachers in educational governments because the teachers stand in the place of the parents (*in loco parentis*): "Now then, my sons, listen to me, and do not depart from the words of my mouth" (Proverbs 5:7). Church members are to obey their pastors, elders, and deacons in ecclesiastical (Church) governments: "Obey your leaders, and submit to them; for they keep watch over your souls, as those who will give an account"

(Hebrews 13:17). Citizens are to obey their rulers in civil governments: "Submit yourselves for the Lord's sake to every human institution, whether to a king as the one in authority, or to governors as sent by him for the punishment of evildoers and the praise of those who do right" (1 Peter 2:13-17).

No matter what the sphere of government—whether in creation or culture, whether through husbands, parents, teachers, Church rulers, or civil authorities—it is God who ultimately governs: "Let every person be in subjection to the governing authorities. For there is no authority except from God, and those which exist are established by God" (Romans 13:1). [I am indebted to Francis Nigel Lee for much of the above material.]

Because men and women are created in the image of God, they are, by nature, governing creatures. They reflect the governing attributes of their Creator. Even after the fall, man's responsibility to govern continued, though affected by sin. Because of the entrance of sin into the created order, the breakdown of all types of governments spread quickly. Family government was disrupted as the husband blamed his wife for his own sin: "The woman whom Thou gavest to be with me, she gave me from the tree, and I ate" (Genesis 3:12). Brother went against brother with murder as the result: "Cain rose up against Abel his brother and killed him" (Genesis 4:8). This was made more evident by the anarchy that prevailed before God's watery judgment: "As a result wickedness became universal and evil was hopelessly ingrained in 'every imagination of the thoughts [Genesis 6:5]'" (*Concordia Self-Study Commentary*, p. 22).

When the breakdown of society occurred, political power was seen as man's "salvation." By changing man's surroundings through political means it was believed that a better world could be created. The results of such an assumption led to tyranny and oppression. Theft, murder, and slavery were often used to usher in this "better world." The confiscation of property was not beyond the tactics of those in positions of power who wanted even more prestige and authority (1 Kings 21). When coercion did not work, murder was always an option (v. 13). Murder was used by some to advance politically. Positions of power could be captured by eliminating the opposition (2 Samuel 3:26-30). Even the citizens are willing to give up their duties under God for the promises of "salvation" through the agency of the state (1 Samuel 8). While civil government at all levels of society is necessary (city, county, state, and national), it must not usurp other legitimate governing authorities ordained by God.

Since God is Creator and Sustainer of all things, it follows that all other governments are subservient to His system of government. The creation does not have priority over the Creator. The creature cannot govern the world according to an arbitrary system of government. Neither can man elevate any one system of government above the fact that God is the supreme government, because "the government rests on His shoulders" (Isaiah 9:6). There is no legitimate government unless it takes its meaning from the God who has the very meaning of government in His character. When men or nations seek to deify any one government over all others, we can expect a total collapse of all other legitimate governments that find their meaning in the only true Governor of the Universe.

As sin increased so did the development of civil government. Since man would not govern himself, and his lack of self-government jeopardized the property and lives of others, God instituted specific governing requirements. Human governments were required by God to punish crimes that threatened life, liberty, and property: "Whoever sheds man's blood, by man shall his blood be shed, for in the image of God He made man" (Genesis 9:6; cf. Exodus 20-24). Defense treaties were made by various family heads because of the potential misunderstandings that could have arisen because of man's sinfulness (see Genesis 14;13; 31:51-52; 34:8-10). Moreover, as families developed into different national entities, international cooperation between various national leaders for the purpose of conducting war or promoting peaceful alliances often developed (see Genesis 14:1-2; 2 Chronicles 17-20).

So He drove the man out; and at the east of the garden of Eden He stationed the cherubim, and the flaming sword which turned every direction, to guard the way to the tree of life (Genesis 3:24).

Questions for Discussion

God as the Supreme Governor

"GOVERNOR, n. He that governs, rules, or directs; one invested with supreme authority. 'The Creator is the rightful *governor* of all his creatures'" (Noah Webster, 1828).

1. Who is the model for all types of governments? Explain. (Psalm 22:28; 47:7-8; 103:19)

_____

_____

_____

_____

_____

2. Who has the ultimate authority to govern? Why? (Jeremiah 27:5; Proverbs 8:15; 21:1; Matthew 28:18

_____

_____

_____

_____

_____

3. Since God is the ultimate authority and Governor, does this mean that all those who rule must do so by acknowledging God's authority and not their own? What happens to those who rule without acknowledging God as the only true sovereign ruler? Explain. (Psalm 99:1-5; Romans 13:1; Daniel 4:31-32)

_____

_____

_____

_____

_____

The Origin of Government

1. Who was given authority to govern? What were they to govern? (Genesis 1:26-28; 2:15-20)

_____

_____

_____

_____

2. What was to be their standard for proper government? Explain. (Genesis 1:26; 2:16-17)

_____

_____

_____

_____

3. How did Adam and Eve fail to exercise self-government? (Genesis 3:1-7, 22)

_____

_____

_____

_____

4. What happened to the world that Adam and Eve were to have governed? (Genesis 3:17-19)

_____

_____

_____

_____

5. What governmental systems remained and even developed after man's fall into sin?

Genesis 3:16

_____

_____

_____

Genesis 4:1

_____
_____
_____
_____

Genesis 4:3-4

_____
_____
_____
_____

Genesis 4:12

_____
_____
_____
_____

Genesis 4:17

_____
_____
_____
_____

Genesis 4:20

_____
_____
_____
_____

Genesis 4:21-22 and Psalm 150:3-6

_____
_____
_____
_____

The Development of Civil Government

1. In this verse, what necessity do you see for external (civil) government? Why? (Genesis 6:1-2)

_____

_____

_____

_____

2. What was the attitude of those choosing wives? What does this attitude suggest about the nature of government at this time? (Genesis 6:2)

_____

_____

_____

_____

3. What authority does man now have to protect life? (Genesis 9:4-6)

_____

_____

_____

_____

4. What evidence is there that government was a universal concept? (Genesis 10:31-32)

_____

_____

_____

_____

_____

5. How did the concept of civil government express itself during the patriarchal period of Israel's history? (Genesis 12:10-20; 13:12; 14:1-16)

_____

_____

_____

6. After Israel's release from Egyptian bondage, what form of governmental (civil) system was instituted? What was the basis for Israel's civil and religious systems? (Exodus 19:4-8; Deuteronomy 29:10-13)

_____

_____

_____

_____

_____

7. How did self, family, and Church (worship) governments deteriorate during the period of the judges? What was God's response to Israel's lack of self-control? (Judges 17:6; 2:10-23)

_____

_____

_____

_____

_____

8. What does Israel's choosing a king to rule over them tell you about the people's faith and trust in God as their "Governor" (King)? (1 Samuel 8:5-9; Deuteronomy 17:14-17)

_____

_____

_____

_____

_____

9. Have God's requirements for proper government changed? If they have not, then what will happen to any society that ignores God's standards for government? (Deuteronomy 31:15-20) Compare what is going on in our nation today with the blessings and the curses of Leviticus 26 and Deuteronomy 28.

_____

_____

_____

_____

_____

Summary

"The story of Cain and Abel shows how early appeared the acute need for coercive restraint on violent impulses by some police action (Gen 4:1-16). There follows the incident of Lamech and his sword-brandishing bravado before his family in a polygamous household (Gen 4:19-24). His boastful song manifests all the madness of armed violent wickedness throughout man's long history. The perversity of 'reeking tube and iron shard, all valiant dust that builds on dust, and guarding calls not thee to guard' (Kipling; *Recessional)* is suggested in those couplet lines, 'Adah and Zillah, hear my voice; Ye wives of Lamech, hearken unto my speech: For I have slain a man for wounding me, And a young man for bruising me: If Cain shall be avenged sevenfold, truly Lamech seventy and sevenfold' (Gen 4:23-24). As a matter of fact, the Genesis narrative relates that it was precisely this tendency to violence, unrestrained by any formal organized social control, that in part brought on the judgment of the deluge, for, 'God said unto Noah, The end of all flesh is come before me; for the earth is filled with violence through them; and, behold, I will destroy them with the earth' (Gen 6:13)...If sin's violence to man cannot be kept in check by voluntary controls [self government], then God in His grace would control it by coercive means." (Robert Duncan Culver, *Toward a Biblical View of Civil Government,* p. 71f.)

And it came about when they were in the field, that Cain rose up against Abel his brother and killed him (Genesis 4

Answers to Questions for Discussion

God as The Supreme Governor

1. God as Governor over all His creation is the pattern and model for all governmental systems. God has given us a record of how He governs in His word; therefore, God's word should be the standard for all our governments.

2. Ultimately, only God has the authority to govern. He does so because He is God, and His infinite wisdom and majesty are beyond compare. He grants authority to others to govern: "By Me kings reign, and rulers decree justice" (Proverbs 8:15). Noah Webster wrote: "The Creator is the rightful *governor* of all his creatures."

3. All who rule receive their authority for the administration of justice and equity from God, Lord (Governor) of all creation. When man seeks to usurp God's ultimate authority, God then shows the creature how dependent he really is: "'King Nebuchadnezzar, to you it is declared: sovereignty has been removed from you, and you will be driven away from mankind and your dwelling place will be with the beasts of the field. You will be given grass to eat like cattle, and seven periods of time will pass over you, until you recognize that the Most High is ruler over the realm of mankind, and He bestows it on whomever He wishes'" (Daniel 4:31-32).

The Origin of Governments

1. Adam and Eve were given authority to govern themselves (Genesis 2:16-17); the garden that God had given them (Genesis 2:15); the animals that God had placed in their care (Genesis 1:28; 2:20); and the earth that He created (Genesis 1:28).

2. Adam and Eve's standard was to reflect God's standard. Because man was created in the image of God, he is to reflect that image in the manner in which he fulfills all his duties (Genesis 1:26). God had given oral commands to instruct them in the way of righteousness (2:16-17). God would later have His directives for the proper administration of government put into writing to be passed down through the generations.

59

3. In terms of self-government Adam and Eve decided to govern themselves according to their own standard of right and wrong. They would decide for themselves what was good and what was evil (Genesis 3:1-7, 22). They would judge whether God's words were true or whether Satan's words were true. By rejecting God's command, they established their desires as the ultimate standard of authority.

4. The world that Adam and Eve were to have dominion over would not be easily governed. Before the fall, the earth and its creatures were without the curse of sin. After the fall, governing would take a great deal more time and would meet with failure on a regular basis, serving as a reminder to Adam and his generations of the results of his great sin. Disobedience has its consequences: "Do not be deceived, God is not mocked; for whatever a man sows, this he will also reap" (Galatians 6:7).

5. [Genesis 3:16] Marriage government was the first relationship to be affected by the fall. Adam blamed Eve for his sin: "The woman whom Thou gavest to be with me, she gave me from the tree, and I ate" (Genesis 3:12). Even after the fall, the marital relationship demands, where two image bearers are united, that one must ultimately rule. But even in this, the husband must rule according to God's law and not his own. The husband's role as governor of his wife in the marriage relationship must never be seen as a license to dominate with force. Husbands should always remember that God is both just and loving (cf. Ephesians 5:21-25).

[Genesis 4:1] Family government begins with the bearing of children. Children are not to be left to their own devices when it comes to the way they should be raised; instead: "Train up a child in the way he should go, even when he is old he will not depart from it" (Proverbs 22:6). Children must be raised according to God's law. When the law of God is set before them as a "tutor," it will lead them to Christ: "Therefore the Law has become our tutor to lead us to Christ, that we may be justified by faith" (Galatians 3:24). Children must be made to understand that their only hope for salvation lies in the perfection and righteousness of Christ. He is to be their Governor.

[Genesis 4:3-4] God's government even rules the principles of worship, and man must govern the affairs of worship according to God's requirements: "Now

A marriage certificate illustrating the biblical duties of husband and wife.

Nadab and Abihu, the sons of Aaron, took their respective fire pans, and after putting fire in them, placed incense on it and offered strange fire before the LORD, which He had not commanded them. And fire came out from the presence of the LORD and consumed them, and they died before the LORD" (Leviticus 10:1-2). If men were free to worship as they pleased, they would be free to worship any object or person as they pleased (cf. Isaiah 44:9-20).

[Genesis 4:12] Man is still to govern creation. The "weeds" (Genesis 3:18) are not to rule him. The results of the curse are to come under the dominion of man as he operates according to God's principles of cultural government.

[Genesis 4:17] Cities must have a godly form of government. The establishment of cities necessitates a government beyond self-government and family government. When two or more families are living in close proximity to one another it becomes necessary to have laws that protect the property and lives of all family members.

[Genesis 4:20] Man is to rule the animal world rather than to be ruled by it. Eve should have realized that something was wrong when a creature questioned her about a command that God had given (Genesis 3:1). The serpent's authority was out of order. Man had dominion over the created order, including the animals. This is made evident when God commanded Adam to name the animals. God was showing Adam that he had proper governing authority over the animals in a way similar to the way God had authority over Adam. God named Adam. Moreover, man is to govern the productivity of the animals. They are to serve man by giving him the resources—beasts of burden, milk, skins for clothing, and so forth—which God has made available in order to lighten the load of the curse.

[Genesis 4:21-22] Man is to govern cultural affairs. No area of culture is free from the Lordship of Jesus Christ. The arts, design, music, and recreation must be governed by man according to the standards of God's holy character. The

Man's creative gifts are to be developed for the glory of the Creator.

form and materials of God's creation make art and beauty possible: human creativity should reflect God's own creative acts. To ignore culture would be to ignore the very design of the universe and its intricate formation. "The best of the traditional view of the Church, supported by biblical teaching, has been (thankfully) that the arts, creativity, enjoyment of our own creativity, the creativity of those around us—in short, all the beauty that God has put into this life—comes as a direct good and gracious gift from our Heavenly Father" (Franky Schaeffer, *Addicted to Mediocrity*, p. 16). To deny these gifts would be to deny the Creator.

The Development of Civil Government

1. The multiplication of peoples necessitates some form of civil government to keep law and order as well as to protect life and property. Because of the multiplication of peoples, there is a multiplication of the natural results of sin. The sinless society of the pre-Fall world gave way to murder, lust, theft, and war as the result of man's depraved nature.

2. The necessity of external restraint is made evident because of the violent nature of those who desired to take wives for themselves. Those taking wives did so without any regard to any law or moral order: "They took wives for themselves, whomever they chose" (Genesis 6:2). When self-government is repudiated, it is the responsibility of civil government to restrain evil. Because of the complete disregard for self- and family government, God determined to exterminate a godless society. By God's grace only eight people survived the flood.

3. Only duly constituted civil authorities, who are ultimately under the government of God, have the legal right and duty to wield the sword to punish evil-doers. No individual is free to take the life of another human being without just biblical cause (e.g., self-defense). God has placed in man's authority the governing responsibility to punish any who would willfully take the life of another.

4. There were family, regional, and national governments. Each of these groups was a relatively autonomous governing body free from the potential despotic rule of other families and clans. Each group was probably aware of other groups and the standards that were set and acknowledged. To transgress the boundary of their law would mean punishment.

5. During Abraham's time, civil government was far-reaching but was probably unofficially organized similar to other prominent families or clans. There were independent city-states (Genesis 13:12) where "kings" were the ruling power. When an outside attack arose, there was a consolidation of power among the various kings for the protection of the occupied area. Even trained family armies (probably organized by clans) were part of the many city-states (Genesis 14:14).

6. Since God was responsible for Israel's deliverance and liberty, the Israelites were, therefore, obligated to obey the covenant that God had established with them. [In any case all nations are obligated to obey God by virtue of His position as Creator and sustainer of all things. Without His aid, no nation could exist.] The covenant declaration made by God to Israel was in fact Israel's "Constitution." The people acknowledged their covenantal obligation with these words: "All that the LORD has spoken we will do!" (Exodus 19:8) Here we have the consent of the people (the governed) responding to the stipulations of the covenant-giver (the Governor), their law-giver and Redeemer. The covenant stipulations were based on the laws revealed to the people from Mount Sinai; therefore, the covenant ("Constitution") was grounded in law and not in the will of the people. To break the covenant was to break the law of the covenant; to break the law of the covenant was to offend the Covenant Maker; to offend the Covenant Maker was to incur His wrath.

7. The period of the Judges exhibits the people of Israel's desire to be their own God: "Every man did what was right in his own eyes" (Judges 17:6). The beginning of Israel's rebellion against God was with the individual. This is the theme of Judges. All subsequent rebellion in the area of government is the result of the individual rebelling. The generation which arose after Joshua's death did not know the Lord who delivered Israel from Egyptian bondage: "And there arose another generation after them who did not know the LORD, nor yet the work which He had done for Israel" (Judges 2:10). Either the parents failed to instruct their children, or the children rebelled against the instruction of the parents. The people then served other gods: "They forsook the LORD, the God of their fathers, who had brought them out of the land of Egypt, and followed other gods from among the gods of the people who were around them" (Judges 2:12). God was provoked to anger: "Wherever they went, the hand of the LORD was against them for evil, as the LORD had spoken and as the LORD had sworn to them, so that they were severely distressed" (Judges 2:15). God in His great mercy raised up Judges (temporal saviors) to deliver the people from foreign oppression (Judges 2:16-18).

8. The people of Israel did not understand that their apostasy was directly related to their oppression by foreign powers, especially the Philistines. Instead of repenting of their sins and turning to God as their true king, they instead demanded an earthly king "to judge [them] like all the nations" (1 Samuel 8:6). Israel looked to a man to save the nation. God was not displeased with the concept of a king. He had earlier promised them that they would have a king: "When you enter the land which the LORD your God gives you, and you possess it and live in it, and you say, 'I will set a king over me like all the nations who are around me,' you shall surely set a king over you whom the LORD your God chooses..." (Deuteronomy 17:14-17). The fault of the people was their desire to have a king who would be their savior. The people had, in fact, rejected God as their king: "They have not rejected you [Samuel], but they have rejected Me from being king over them" (1 Samuel 8:7).

9. The requirements for godly civil government have not changed. God sets before all nations life and death, the blessing and the curse: "See, I have set before you today life and prosperity, and death and adversity; in that I command you today to love the LORD your God, to walk in His ways and to keep His commandments and His statutes and His judgments, that you may live and multiply, and the LORD your God may bless you...I have set before you life and death, the blessing and the curse. So choose life in order that you may live, you and your descendants, by loving the LORD your God, by obeying His voice, and by holding fast to Him; for this is your life and the length of your days" (Deuteronomy 30:15-16, 19-20).

The American flag, symbol of a federated union of sovereign states. *Resolved: that the flag of the United States of America be 13 stripes alternate red and white, that the union be 13 stars, white in a blue field representing a new constellation* (June 3, 1777).

Lesson 4

The Purpose
and Function of
Civil Government

As we have seen in the previous lessons, there are different forms and functions of governments performing specified governing tasks, from the individual to the state. Since this lesson is concerned with civil government, it is our task to establish its obligations and limits of authority. By now it should be evident that the creature has no authority or power to dictate or to establish the requirements of civil government. This responsibility belongs to the One who established the realm of civil government; therefore, its authority should not extend beyond the requirements set by God. This means that the state is not to operate in the areas of the family, school, or Church if the Bible makes no provision for the civil government's power and authority in these areas.

Because of a lack of understanding and sound teaching many people are not aware of the purpose and function of civil government's authority. Many people assume that the national government has absolute authority because it claims the authority for itself. The claim of authority does not validate the claim. No government is autonomous, a law unto itself. This is as true for the state as it is for the family, school, and Church.

All authority and its limitations are delegated. No one government can claim its area of governmental authority as ultimate. Neither can any one governmental authority validate or invalidate another legitimate governmental authority. God is the only ultimate authority. He determines the proper function of any legitimate authority structure. Moreover, He establishes the limitations of these same governing authorities. If any authority sets itself up as the absolute authority, it has replaced the ultimate authority of God. The

Apostle Paul has stated it clearly: "There is no authority except from God, and those which exist are established by God" (Romans 13:1). "This is a very comprehensive proposition. All authority is of God. No man has any rightful power over other men, which is not derived from God. All human power is delegated and ministerial. This is true of parents, of magistrates, and of church officers" (Charles Hodge, *A Commentary on Romans*, p. 406).

There is no authority except from God, and those which exist are established by God (Romans 13:1). All authority is of God. No man has any rightful power over other men, which is not derived from God. All human power is delegated and ministerial.

–Charles Hodge

In the area of civil government, it is crucial to understand the question of the source and function of governmental authority. The authority of any system of thought is the god of that system. If a national government establishes the will of the people, an elected elite, a law court, or an individual as the ultimate authority, that is the nation's god. If the source of authority is the voice of the people, then the people are the gods of that nation (*vox populi; vox Dei*—"The voice of the people is the voice of God"). If a nation's source of authority is a court, then the court has established itself as that nation's god. If there is no authority beyond man, then man has become god. When a nation chooses its authority, it has chosen its god.

Too often, however, people decide who they want to be their authority rather than acknowledge the absolute authority of God. But in rejecting the one authority, they accept another authority. Two choices are set before a nation. Either God is the ultimate authority or man is. "No man can escape the problem of authority. Every man will consciously or unconsciously appeal to some authority as basic and ultimate to life. Most authorities revered by men today are human authorities: the individual, the people, the elite thinkers and planners, science, reason, or the state, these are all humanistic authorities" (R.J. Rushdoony, *Law and Liberty*, p. 32). The sad thing is that people choose these authorities to govern them without ever realizing that when man is set up as the ultimate authority tyranny soon follows. The people choose such despotic authorities because they believe those who govern will abundantly supply them with their desires. The unrestrained growth of the federal government in our day is partly the result of citizens' desires and expectations. Harold O.J. Brown has said it well:

Unless we control our appetites, we cannot control our government. We certainly cannot expect it to limit itself, because it senses our appetites far more strongly than it is persuaded by our claims that we are tired of bureaucracy, taxes, and government interference. If the ultimate goal of government is to 'do everything and change everything,' really an infinite challenge, then it will require an infinite effort—in fact, infinite taxes, infinite paperwork, and infinite interference: infinite in the sense that there will be no limit to them, no place at which people will say, 'This is clearly all that we want or need,' until the limits of exhaustion are reached. *Infinite goals mean infinite controls.* And infinite controls mean zero freedom (*The Reconstruction of the Republic*, p. 87).

If citizens do not become aware of the intended biblical function of civil government, two things will happen. First, individuals, families, churches, and schools will lay aside their God-ordained responsibilities. The result will be that the civil government with its ever-growing bureaucracy will take on the responsibilities reserved for the citizens at the expense of their freedoms. Second, those who function in the realm of civil government will tyrannize and exploit the governed by controlling their lives with laws never meant to be used by the civil authorities.

If we are to define the limits of civil government, the word of God must be our source. The purpose, function, and authority of civil government are clearly developed in the pages of Scripture. No individual or group of individuals is at liberty to change the limits within which civil governments should rule.

United States Capitol.

Questions for Discussion

1. What must all rulers and citizens be aware of when they consider the establishment of the purpose and function of governmental systems? (Daniel 5:21; Romans 13:1; Psalm 83:18; Psalm 127:1)

_____

_____

_____

_____

_____

_____

2. What powers has God given to civil government in order for it to carry out its responsibilities effectively? (Romans 13:4; Genesis 9:5-7)

_____

_____

_____

_____

_____

_____

3. What title is given to those who govern? (Romans 13:4)

_____

_____

4. Do all rulers live up to this title of honor, and if they do not, why does Paul, through inspiration from the Holy Spirit, give them the title "minister"? (Luke 13:31-32; Acts 2:22-23; 12:1-4)

_____

_____

_____

_____

_____

_____

5. What does being a "minister of God" mean? How should the "ministry" of our civil government function? (Luke 22:24-27; Matthew 20:20-28; 1 Peter 4:10-11; Acts 20:34; Philippians 2:25; Hebrews 6:10)

_____

_____

_____

_____

_____

_____

6. "Rulers are not a cause of fear for good behavior, but for evil [behavior]" (Romans 13:3). How do rulers distinguish what is "good" from what is "evil"? (Romans 7:12; 16:19; 1 Timothy 1:8; Hebrews 5:14; 3 John 11)

_____

_____

_____

_____

_____

7. Should a ruler establish laws according to his own personal (subjective) standard of good and evil? (Isaiah 5:20; Proverbs 17:15)

_____

_____

_____

_____

_____

8. What are some additional duties that civil governments should perform and for what purpose? (1 Timothy 2:1-2; 1 Peter 2:13-17)

_____

_____

_____

_____

_____

_____

9. Compare the above "duties" to those of our present civil governments (federal, state, county, and city). How do present-day rulers compare with the biblical ideal? Cite some examples in the areas of education, religion, courts, etc.

_____

_____

_____

_____

_____

10. Concerning taxation, how is it determined "what is due" civil governments? (1 Samuel 8)

_____

_____

_____

_____

11. According to Romans 13:6-7, what is the citizen's financial responsibility to the civil government? For what purpose is the collected tax to be used?

_____

_____

_____

_____

Summary

"All power is ordained of God, and the state is one such power. Man's law must be rooted in God's law; lawlessness in this sense is resistance to God. First of all, civil government is of divine institution. It is ordained of God and is a part of God's kingdom and government (Rom. 13:1,2). Second, civil government is ordained to promote good by providing conditions for its welfare by punishing criminals and preventing crime. Its essential function is thus justice, godly order (Rom. 13:3,4). Third, civil government has the approval of Christian conscience. It is an authority, like that of parents and church officers, which is ordained of God, the only rightful source of authority" (R.J. Rushdoony, _Politics of Guilt and Pity_, p. 336).

Answers to Questions for Discussion

1. All rulers and citizens must be aware that the establishment of authority and power among rulers and nations is the result of God's sovereign decree, according to His good pleasure. No civil government can claim that it has risen by its own strength and wisdom; to do so is to bring the wrath and judgment of God upon the whole nation. "And if a sparrow can not fall to the ground without His notice, is it probable that an empire can rise without His aid?" (Benjamin Franklin's address to the Constitutional Convention of 1787) "Unless the Lord builds the house, they labor in vain who build it" (Psalm 127:1).

2. God has established civil government to be an avenger who brings (God's) wrath upon those who practice evil. The civil government's power to use the sword is legitimate in certain limited cases. The Bible has mandated that the power of the sword is to keep the peace, to protect those who do what is right.

3. Rulers are said to be ministers of God.

4. Not all rulers live up to the honorable title of "minister." Paul is speaking of the ideal. Rulers are in fact ministers, regardless of how they rule, because God designates them as such (Romans 13:1). The question is whether or not they are performing their ministry in a way that is consistent with God's word. Not everyone who claims the title of "minister" is really ministering in the biblical sense: "Be on guard for yourselves and for all the flock...I know that after my departure savage wolves will come in among you, not sparing the flock; and from among your own selves men will arise, speaking perverse things, to draw away the disciples after them" (Acts 20:28-30). In the same way, not every ruler who seizes power or who is elected to office will, in fact, minister (e.g., Pontius Pilate, Herod, Hitler, etc.). Paul is describing what a ruler's proper function is. The apostle is not making a moral judgment about any particular ruler or political policy. Rather, his words describe what civil governments ought to be and ought to do. Every ruler should seek to minister as Christ ministered. Notice that Jesus calls Herod "that fox" (Luke 13:32). Jesus did not approve of Herod wanting to kill Him, and He said so. Jesus was not calling the legitimacy of civil government into question, but He was making a value judgment about Herod who held the office of governor. Jesus was informing the people that Herod was sly; therefore, they were to be on their guards when dealing with him. To remain silent when an evil is being committed is to have a hand in the evil.

5. For many, being a minister means being a dictator. The typical ruler of Jesus' day was a tyrant. "The kings of the Gentiles lord it over them [the people]" (Luke 22:25). The greatest example of "lording it over" a people was the tyrannical government of Rome. The distinguishing characteristic of true leadership is that of being a servant. A minister in the biblical sense always places the welfare of others first. The ministry of the civil government does not exist to serve its own needs. Civil governments do not exist for their own end. The true minister (servant) exists to serve others, but never apart from the laws of God. In the case of the civil magistrate, the duties of service are spelled out by Paul in Romans 13:3-4 and other places in Scripture.

6. The rulers in the realm of civil government, who are ministers of God, must rule according to God's law, the standard of good and evil. No government has the freedom to rule by some arbitrary man-centered standard of good and evil. The state is a true minister when it operates according to biblical absolutes.

7. No ruler or group of rulers has the authority to establish any law that is in opposition to the laws of God. Since God's word is the standard for good and evil, no man or civil government can institute any law contrary to the unchanging law of God; therefore, any law that is put into effect that is not biblical in nature is evil. Moreover, the state cannot claim "neutrality" in the area of law. All law is a declaration of morality; therefore, law is religious in nature. For rulers to declare that God's laws are not legitimate is to say that only man's laws are.

8. The additional duties of civil governments are the well ordering of society and the maintaining of peace so that Christians are free to worship God, unhindered by forces hostile to the gospel of Jesus Christ. The state has the duty to preserve law and order so that the Church is free to spread the gospel of peace. The civil government must be made to realize that there is no real peace without the presence of the Spirit of Jesus Christ. This climate of peace can only

It is the duty of the civil magistrate to protect these who do good so *that we may lead a tranquil and quiet life in all godliness and dignity* (1 Timothy 2:2)

be accomplished by administering justice and righteousness. Justice and righteousness are defined in terms of God's law. Civil rulers are commissioned to represent God as the Judge. They act in such a capacity when they punish those who do evil (i.e., break God's laws), as well as publicly commend and reward those who do good (cf. Romans 13:3-4).

9. This answer is to be your own.

10. Even taxation by the state must be determined by the word of God. Because the function of civil government is limited to the administration of justice, rewarding good behavior, and punishing lawlessness, the tax requirement is to be small. Only when the civil government extends its limits of authority beyond the biblical directive—education, welfare, the arts, etc.—does the tax bite increase. A civil government may not usurp powers or invade other governmental spheres (family, Church, school, business) not assigned to it by

God unless a crime (designated by biblical law) has been committed. (See NOTE below explaining the limitations of civil government's authority in the area of criminal justice.)

11. The civil government has the authority and power to collect a tax for certain services that it renders. But as we have seen, the only services that civil magistrates are to render are those that administer justice, protect law-abiding citizens, and punish the lawless. If the civil government is performing duties beyond those specified by Scripture, then it is overstepping its legitimate authority.

NOTE [Answer 10]: The Bible makes a distinction between sins and crimes. Not all crimes are sins, and not all sins are crimes. There are sins of the heart that may not express themselves in outward actions. Strife, jealousy, envy, anger, resentment, and lust are sins which cannot be punished by civil authorities because human authorities have no way of judging the heart. There are, however, times when sins manifest themselves outwardly and become crimes: "You have heard that the ancients were told, 'You shall not commit murder [a crime]' and 'Whoever commits murder shall be liable to the court'" (Matthew 5:21). The inward expression of the heart, hate, expressed itself in an outward action, murder. Both hate and murder are sins but only one (murder) is a crime. While citizens can only be punished by the state for crimes, citizens are always liable before God for sins. Hate and murder fall into the category of sins before God.

Crimes are not always sins, however. The civil magistrate (the state) may declare certain actions to be criminal: "They [the authorities] commanded them [James and John] not to speak or teach at all in the name of Jesus" (Acts 4:18; cf. Exodus 1:15-22; 2:1-10; Joshua 2; Daniel 1, 3 and 6). Obeying "God rather than men" (Acts 5:29) may be "criminal" in the eyes of the state, but such "criminality" is not sinful in the eyes of God: "Whether it is right in the sight of God to give heed to you rather than to God, you be the judge; for we cannot stop speaking what we have seen and heard" (Acts 4:19-20). Therefore, the state's authority to punish those who do evil only includes crimes that are designated as such by the word of God.

In the eyes of the State, during the first century, acknowledging Jesus Christ as Lord was often a crime punishable by death. Those who died, however, looked for a more secure home and state—a dwelling with God—something the civil State attempts to imitate in utopian fashion.

I am the LORD, that is My name; I will not give My glory to another, nor My praise to graven images (Isaiah 42:8).

Lesson 5

The Biblical Form of Civil Government

A brief survey of the Bible and its principles will show that it has directives for all areas of life. Does this, however, include civil government? Is God as concerned about the structure and principles of political systems as He is about families? Or, has God left the area of political systems for man to develop according to the needs of a particular era or to satisfy the desires of a particular people? Or, does the Bible claim "neutrality" in certain areas of life, leaving man to create his own directives? For example, is there a Christian economic system? Or, is the study of economics a neutral enterprise? Does the Bible set forth directives in the area of science? Are there certain creational laws that God has established to order the universe? Is it possible to develop an educational system from Scripture? Can educational facts have any meaning if they are not related to God and His word? Can one really be "educated" if Christ is not at the center of his life giving meaning to all facts and experiences? Are there commandments that address the issues of business?

The Bible clearly teaches that Jesus is Lord and that His lordship extends over all of society's institutions, including the family, economics, science, education, and for this study, civil government. There is no realm of society where the lordship of Jesus Christ can be ignored. When political systems rule, they rule in accordance with a law system. This is inevitable. There can be no neutral law system. "It must be recognized that in any culture, the source of law is the god of that society" (R.J. Rushdoony, *Institutes of Biblical Law*, p. 4). If man is the source of a society's laws, then man is the god of that society. If society ignores the governing principles that God has set forth in His word, then that society is competing with the Lord of all creation. But Scripture is clear; God does not compete with His creation: "That they may know that Thou alone, whose name is the LORD, art the Most High over all the earth" (Psalm 83:18). God shares His glory with no man, society, or political system: "I am the LORD, that is My name; I will not give My glory to another, nor My praise to graven images" (Isaiah 42:8; 48:11).

A Christian is just as much under obligation to obey God's will in the most secular of his daily businesses as he is in his [prayer] closet or at the communion table. He has no right to separate his life into two realms, and acknowledge different moral codes in each respectively— God reigns over all.... His will is the supreme law in all relations and actions.

–A.A. Hodge

There are many who would say that the Bible has no business in the so-called secular realm. The Bible is useful for spiritual matters but not the substantive matters of civil government, law, economics, politics, and science. Times have changed and the Bible is an out-of-date book. So say many in our day. But the Christian has the duty to follow the only true King and the commandments of His kingdom. If we truly love Jesus Christ, we must follow His commandments. When His commandments speak to civil government, we must obey. A.A. Hodge, the great Princeton theologian of a century ago, had this to say about the Christian's duty to obey Jesus Christ in all areas of life, including civil government:

> A Christian is just as much under obligation to obey God's will in the most secular of his daily businesses as he is in his closet [in prayer] or at the communion table. He has no right to separate his life into two realms, and acknowledge different moral codes in each respectively—to say the Bible is a good rule for Sunday, but this is a week-day question; or the Scriptures are the right rule in matters of religion, but this is a question of business or of politics. God reigns

over all everywhere. His will is the supreme law in all relations and actions. His inspired Word, loyally read, will inform us of His will in every relation and act of life, secular as well as religious; and the man is a traitor who refuses to walk therein with scrupulous care. The kingdom of God includes all sides of human life, and it is a kingdom of absolute righteousness. You are either a loyal subject or a traitor. When the King comes, how will he find you doing? (A.A. Hodge, *Evangelical Theology*, pp. 280-281)

To deny that there is a biblical system of civil government is to say that God has no standard of righteousness and justice in this crucial area. If men and nations can pick and choose the system of civil government they desire, man becomes ultimate and God becomes subordinate to man's desires. How could a system of civil government ever be evaluated if the system is arbitrary at the very start? If a group of disenchanted citizens wished to overthrow the first arbitrary government, what standard of justice would prohibit them from doing it? If any man-made governmental system is legitimate, then it follows that all man-made governmental systems are legitimate. Those who have the means, the power, and the influence are the ones who rule. Because all of life is to reflect the character of God, we must expect civil government to reflect His character as well. No two competing systems of civil government can be right. Only the Bible can be our guide in determining which is right. The experiences of history and the desires of men are of little consequence if they do not support or reflect the system of civil government outlined in Scripture. "To the law and to the testimony! If they do not speak according to this word, it is because they have no dawn" (Isaiah 8:19-20).

Hear, O Israel, the statutes and the ordinances which I am speaking today in your hearing, that you may learn them and observe them carefully (Deuteronomy 5:1).

Questions for Discussion

Forms of Civil Government

What form should the ideal government assume in this day of many opinions? Listed below are some of the forms of civil government that have existed or now exist. In your own words, describe each one. Scripture verses have been supplied to help you formulate an answer.

1. Anarchy: Judges 17:6; Deuteronomy 12:8

_____

_____

_____

_____

_____

2. Autocracy: 1 Samuel 8; 1 Kings 12:1-15; 9:15; Matthew 2:16; Exodus 1:8-22; Daniel 3:8-18

_____

_____

_____

_____

_____

_____

3. Communism: Exodus 20:15; Deuteronomy 19:14; 27:17; 1 Kings 21:1-16

_____

_____

_____

_____

_____

_____

_____

4. Democracy: Exodus 23:2; Numbers 13; 14:1-10; 1 Samuel 8:19-22; Luke 23:13-25; Revelation 13:3-8

---

5. Bureaucracy: 1 Kings 12:1-15

---

6. Constitutional Monarchy: Deuteronomy 17:14-20; 31:9-13

---

7. Constitutional Republic: Proverbs 11:14; 24:6; Romans 13:1; Proverbs 15:22

The Biblical Form of Civil Government

At this point, it is necessary to present the biblical ideal to see how the above political systems meet the scriptural standards. Before the Exodus of Israel from Egypt, governing institutions centered around the family (Genesis 14:13; 31:13-52; 34:8-10) and tribes (Exodus 1:1-6). Families and tribes retained governing responsibilities within the immediate family or tribe of which each family was a part. It was not until Moses' appointed term of leadership that the establishment of rule over a variety of tribes developed. This situation later grew to national proportions.

At the time of the Exodus, two problems existed for the people of Israel. First, there was no court system to handle judicial matters. God, through the instrument of Moses' father-in-law, Jethro, established an orderly judicial system. Second, a published law was needed so that an unchanging standard of righteousness would be before the people and the rulers at all times. The published law would give the people a standard by which they could evaluate their lives and their leaders. Both these needs were met in Exodus 18-24.

Exodus 18 presents the biblical model for all civil governments.

1. What difficulty did Moses and the people have in handling judicial matters? (Exodus 18:13)

_____

_____

_____

_____

_____

_____

2. What was the extent of the judgments Moses made on behalf of the people? (Exodus 18:16)

_____

_____

_____

_____

_____

_____

3. What standard did Moses use to make sound judgments between those who had disputes? (Exodus 18:16)

_____

_____

_____

_____

_____

4. What was Jethro's counsel to Moses? (Exodus 18:17-18)

_____

_____

_____

_____

5. Was it proper for Moses to follow the advice of Jethro? Why, or why not? Was Jethro a wise, godly counselor whose word was to be respected? Explain why, or why not. (Exodus 18:12)

_____

_____

_____

_____

_____

_____

_____

6. What procedures did Jethro recommend? There are at least six. (Exodus 18:19-21)

_____

_____

_____

_____

_____

_____

_____

_____

7. What qualifications were required of those who ruled? What implications do these requirements have for those who rule today? (Exodus 18:21)

_____

_____

_____

_____

_____

_____

_____

_____

8. In reference to the citizens, what does Exodus 18:21 assume?

_____

_____

_____

_____

_____

_____

9. According to biblical standards, what characteristics should a contemporary civil government display? Formulate your answer by evaluating your own local, state, and national governments.

_____

_____

_____

_____

_____

_____

_____

_____

Summary

"All political government, whether at the local or municipal level, the regional or state level, or the national or federal level, ultimately derives its authority not from the consent of the governed (thus Jefferson) but from the pleasure of Almighty God (thus Scripture). This is not to say that political governments should not consult their subjects; but this is to say that the authority of the human power-wielder in the last analysis comes from God above and not from the governed beneath. For 'the most high God rules in the Kingdom of men, and He appoints over it whomsoever He wills' (Daniel 5:21)" (Francis Nigel Lee, "Power, Government and State," *Man and His Culture*, p. 67).

Give me now wisdom and knowledge, that I may go out and come in before this people; for who can rule this great people of Thine? (2 Chronicles 1:10)

87

Answers to Questions for Discussion

Forms of Civil Government

1. [Anarchy] Anti-government. The individual is a rule (law) unto himself. There is no higher law, whether it be another man's or God's, that he is obligated to keep. In reality, he is his own god. Modern day terrorism is anarchist in nature. Terrorists acknowledge no legitimate governing authority. They offer no plan after the terror is over: "What are the goals of the terrorists? I wonder if they know. What must be understood by anyone who wishes to make sense of their rhetoric is that the ideal of social justice is only the backdrop for their real commitment, namely, revolution. Revolution is its own goal, its own justification. We are dealing with the religion of revolution..." (Gary North, *Successful Investing in An Age of Envy*, p. 211).

2. [Autocracy] The absolute rule by a monarch or dictator. The individual in power is uncontrolled and has unlimited authority. If he wishes to turn a nation by his decree, the people have no way to resist him except by force. This makes for an unstable nation. The dictator's word is law. The divine right of kings, as practiced by the Stuarts in seventeenth-century England and by Louis XIV and his successors in France, was founded on the belief that the king possessed an absolute grant of authority from God Himself. The divine right theory, therefore, puts the king *above* the law. The fallen nature of man rules out the possibility that any one individual would be able to govern absolutely. God is the only true Autocrat because His nature is perfect and His knowledge is comprehensive.

3. [Communism] Total control of state and society by a single non-elected authoritarian group or party. The individual exists to serve the state (contrast Romans 13:1-7 where rulers are to be "ministers"). Control of all aspects of society is by force. "Communism is a philosophy of life [a world-view], a call to revolutionary action, an organization, armed might, an international conspiracy and a goal" (James D. Bales, *Communism: Its Faith and Fallacies*, pp. 17-18). "Communism is a world-wide political organization advocating: (1) the abolition of all forms of religion; (2) the destruction of private property and the abolition of inheritance; (3) absolute social and racial equality; (4) revolution under the leadership of the Communist International; (5) engaging in activities in foreign countries in order to cause strikes, riots, sabotage, bloodshed, and civil war; (6) destruction of all forms of representative or democratic government, including civil liberties such as freedom of speech, of the press, and of assemblage; (7) the ultimate objective of world revolution to establish the dictatorship of the so-called proletariat into a universal union of soviet socialist republics with its capital in Moscow; (8) the achievement of these ends through extreme appeals to hatred" *(Investigation of Un-American Activities and Propaganda,* House Resolution 282, Union Calendar No. 2, House Report, No. 2, 1939, p. 12). The goals of Communism are listed for us in *The Communist Manifesto:*

(1) Abolition of property in land and application of all rents of land to public purposes.

(2) A heavy progressive or graduated income tax.

(3) Abolition of all right of inheritance.

(4) Confiscation of the property of all emigrants and rebels.

(5) Centralization of credit in the hands of the State, by means of a national bank with State capital and an exclusive monopoly.

(6) Centralization of the means of communication and transport in the hands of the State.

(7) Extension of factories and instruments of production owned by the State; the bringing into cultivation of waste lands, and the improvement of the soil generally in accordance with a common plan.

(8) Equal liability of all to labor. Establishment of industrial armies, especially for agriculture.

(9) Combination of agriculture with manufacturing industries: gradual aboli-

tion of the distinction between town and country, by a more equable distribution of the population over the country.

(10) Free education for all children in public schools. Abolition of children's factory labor in its present form. Combination of education with industrial production, etc.

4. [Democracy] Government directly by the people with rule by the majority. This is the law of majority opinion, "the dictatorship of the 51%" (Francis Schaeffer, *The Church at the End of the 20th Century*, p. 33f.). Absolutes are found in the will of the people, not in God's eternal laws. When the desires of the people change so do the laws. Many Americans are under the illusion that America was founded as a Democracy. This is not true. The United States Constitution makes it clear that we are a republic: "The United States shall guarantee to every State in this Union a Republican Form of Government" (*Article IV, section 4*). The following paragraph deals with the nature and dangers of democracies. The information is taken from an official United States publication (*U.S. War Department, Training Manual No. 2000-25*, November 30, 1928). This publication was withdrawn from the Government Printing Office and the Army posts and was to be suppressed and destroyed without explanation: "Democracy: A government of the masses. Authority derived through mass meeting or any other form of 'direct' expression. Results in mobocracy [mob rule]. Attitude toward property is communistic—negating property rights. Attitude toward law is that the will of the majority shall regulate, whether it be based upon deliberation or governed passion, prejudice, and impulse, without restraint or regard to consequences. Results in demagogism [trying to stir up the people by appeals to emotion, prejudice, etc., in order to establish a new leader], license, agitation, discontent, anarchy." Our nation was founded as a Republic [see No. 6 below], not as a Democracy.

5. [Bureaucracy] The rule or manipulation of a people by non-elected officials and civil servants. As a civil government grows and assumes additional governing responsibilities, it must appoint governing officials to implement the additional services. A bureaucracy can make laws independent of any established system of law, and the electorate cannot remove the bureaucrats from their appointed positions of authority (e.g., the Internal Revenue Service).

90

Rehoboam had certain appointed officials, bureaucrats, who made public policy to the detriment of the nation (1 Kings 12:8-11). The elders were probably elected officials (verses 6-8), while the "certain young men who grew up with" Rehoboam were probably appointed.

6. [Constitutional Monarchy] Israel had a Constitutional Monarchy from the time of King Saul to the time of the exile. The constitution of Israel was the law of God: "Now it shall come about when he [the king] sits on the throne of his kingdom, he shall write for himself a copy of this law on a scroll in the presence of the Levitical priests..." (Deuteronomy 17:18). The monarch, the king, was bound by the constitution, the law. He was to "read it all the days of his life" (v. 19). The people were bound by the same constitution. Every seven years they were reminded of the stipulations of the constitution: "You shall read this law in front of all Israel...the men and the women and the alien who is in your town, in order that they may hear and learn and fear the LORD your God, and be careful to observe all the words of this law" (Deuteronomy 31:11-12).

Too often, however, the king and the people ignored and eventually were ignorant of the constitution. For a time the law was lost. When the Temple was being renovated during the reign of King Josiah the law was not in the hands of the king or the people. It was only after Hilkiah the high priest began to refurbish the Temple that the law was found: "I have found the book of the law in the house of the LORD" (2 Kings 22:8). When the law was read before all the people (2 Kings 23:1-3), the king instituted reforms based on the commands set forth in the law. The people also entered into the covenant (constitution) with the king: "And the king stood by the pillar and made a covenant before the LORD, to walk after the LORD, and to keep His commandments and His testimonies and His statutes with all his heart and all his soul, to carry out the words of this covenant that were written in this book. And all the people entered into the covenant" (v. 3).

Was Israel's Constitutional Monarchy to be a permanent form of government? First, the idea of a law-constitution is certainly permanent because the law is a reflection of the eternal character of God. To do away with the law-constitution would mean that man would be free to establish his own law-constitution. Law would then be arbitrary and subject to change at any moment. The idea of a constitution based on law is basic to any contemporary system of government. Second, government by a king was typological for Israel.

The king typified the coming King, Jesus Christ. God raised up a king in Israel for the people to have an earthly representation of their true King who was to come. Their true King was coming to them (cf. Zechariah 9:9; Matthew 21:5). The rule of earthly kings is temporary, while the rule of Christ the King is eternal: "His kingdom is an everlasting kingdom, and His dominion is from generation to generation" (Daniel 4:3). God's appointed earthly king was David from whom the Messiah would come. Matthew's gospel begins by identifying the link between David and Jesus: "The book of the genealogy of Jesus Christ, the son of David..."(1:1). Therefore the kingship of Israel was fulfilled in Jesus Christ and we no longer seek to establish earthly kings.

There are certain advantages to a monarchy. The king was able to unify the diverse tribes of Israel. In time of war this would be most helpful. The king could muster the forces of the relatively independent tribes to protect the common borders of the nation. The primary duty of the President of the United States is to command the armed forces. The separate states need a way to consolidate their power against a common enemy. Our republican form of civil government reflects this advantage by giving the executive branch authority regarding military decisions. It was no coincidence that our first president, George Washington, was also a military leader. There are also dangers attached to rule by a single man, however. If he becomes corrupt then he can direct the people along an ungodly path. The dangers are similar to that of an autocracy. Again, the Constitutional Republic seeks to remedy the potential corruption by balancing the powers among three branches, the executive, the judicial, and the legislative. More will be said of this in Lesson 8.

7. [Constitutional Republic] Government through elected representatives. It is the privilege and duty of the people to elect their representatives. Constitutional checks and balances and the divisions of powers among federal, state, and local subdivisions are fundamental to this system of civil government. A document, in the form of a covenant (Constitution), is the means by which a system of law is to be implemented. "Republic: Authority is derived through the election by the people of public officials best fitted to represent them [Exodus 18:21]. Attitude toward property is respect for laws and individual rights [Exodus 20:15], and a sensible economic procedure. Attitude toward law is the administration of justice in accord with fixed principles and established evidences, with a strict regard to consequences [Deuteronomy 17:8-13]. A greater number of citizens and extent of territory may be brought within its compass. Avoids the dangerous extreme of either tyranny or mobocracy. Results in statesmanship, liberty, reason, justice, contentment, and progress....Our Constitutional fathers, familiar with the strength and weakness of both autocracy and democracy, with fixed principles definitely in mind, defined a representative republican form of government. They 'made a very marked distinction between a republic and a democracy*** and said repeatedly and emphatically that they had founded a republic'" (U.S. *War Department, Training Manual No. 2000-25*, November 30, 1928).

The Old House of Representatives

The Biblical Form of Civil Government

1. All of Moses' time was being taken up as.he sat to judge the people. The people who had to wait for judgment were unproductive during their wait. Notice the phrase "from the morning until the evening."

2. The implication is that Moses made judgments between two parties who could not resolve the problem themselves.

3. Clearly Moses used the standard of God's law as the system of right judgment in resolving disputes between two parties.

4. Moses had undertaken an impossible task. As the nation grew it would become increasingly more difficult for Moses to be an efficient judge. All his time would be spent in civil affairs.

5. Yes, it was proper for Moses to consider Jethro's advice. When Jethro heard all that the LORD had done at the expense of the Egyptians, he "rejoiced over all the goodness which the LORD had done to Israel" (Exodus 18:9). Jethro then shows his allegiance to God: "Then Jethro, Moses' father-in-law, took a burnt offering and sacrifices for God, and Aaron came with all the elders of Israel to eat a meal with Moses' father-in-law before God" (Exodus 18:12). Through the inspiration of the Holy Spirit, Jethro, a servant of the LORD, presented to Moses sound advice for the ordering of the nation. Jethro was not a pagan. He was a believer in the sovereign LORD of all creation; therefore, his word was to be respected.

6. (1) The people were to be taught "the statutes and laws."

(2) Representatives were to be chosen from the people.

(3) The representatives chosen were to have certain qualifications.

(4) There was to be a division of powers: "and you shall place these (men with the qualifications) over them (the people who are taught "the statutes and laws"), as leaders of thousands (national), of hundreds (regional), of fifties (county), and of tens (local community)."

(5) Their rule was to be "at all times."

(6) Disputes that could not be handled through the representatives would be judged by Moses.

7. Those who rule should be "able men." They should have proved themselves in some form of enterprise. The implication is that they are not to be professional politicians. They should "fear God." They ultimately must answer to God; therefore, they should not fear the people or play the role of a politician, making judgments in order to please the people. The rulers should be "men of truth, those who hate dishonest gain." Their dealings in business should be above reproach. No amount of financial gain promised to them by unscrupulous men should persuade them to follow a course contrary to the laws of God.

8. The only way an individual would know if a man met these qualifications was if he knew the man. This passage assumes that the representative is in contact with the people as he pursues his daily affairs. He must prove himself as a faithful and obedient servant of God. The responsibility of the populace is to observe and evaluate his way of life.

9. This answer is to be your own.

Leadership, especially in a judicial setting, requires godly men who can be trusted to know and apply God's law with diligence, consistency, and justice. Anything less than these qualities will result in a tyranny of the worst kind.

Jesus therefore came out, wearing a crown of thorns and the purple robe. And Pilate said to them, "Behold, the Man!" (Jo 19:5)

Lesson 6

Jesus and
Civil Government

The study of civil government would be incomplete if we did not consider the teaching of Jesus. Since Jesus is Immanuel, "God with us" (Matthew 1:23; Isaiah 7:14; cf. John 1:1, 14), we should not expect Him to deviate from the system of truth set forth in the Old Testament. Too often, however, Jesus is seen in just such a light. He is viewed as a new lawgiver, one who has come to establish a new law order, to break from the system of law that was Israel's beacon to the nations (cf. Deuteronomy 4:5-8). Much of this misunderstanding comes from a misreading of the New Testament.

It is true that Jesus "did away with" certain aspects of the Old Testament law. Those laws dealing with redemption (especially those laws having reference to the shedding of blood) have been done away with in their outward form. This does not mean, however, that the shedding of blood is no longer required by God. Salvation can only come through the shedding of blood: "And according to the Law, one may almost say, all things are cleansed with blood, and without shedding of blood there is no forgiveness" (Hebrews 9:22; cf. Leviticus 17:11). While the "blood of bulls to take away sin" is no longer required, the shedding of blood has not been done away with (cf. Hebrews 10:1-18). Even though the outward form has changed, the requirement of blood has not. The law was never to be a means by which an individual obtains righteousness, but it has always been a standard by which we measure righteousness. In the area of civil government, if the law is done away with, then what will be the standard for righteousness? If it is not the law of God then it will be the law of men.

What should the Christian's response be to the moral and civil laws set forth in the Old Testament? Should they be followed, or have they been abrogated? Jesus answers the question for us. "Do not think that I came to abolish the Law and the Prophets; I did not come to abolish, but to fulfill. For truly I say to you, until heaven and earth pass away, not the smallest letter or stroke shall pass away from the Law, until all is accomplished" (Matthew 5:17-18). It was not the purpose of Jesus to write a new moral code. Since the law is a reflection of God's eternal character, we should expect its continuing validity.

The Sermon on the Mount is often interpreted as Jesus' reappraisal of the Old Testament system of law rather than as an evaluation of the application of the law as it was interpreted by the Pharisees. This can be demonstrated by a study of a very familiar, and frequently misunderstood, passage of Scripture. "You have heard that it was said, 'An eye for an eye, and a tooth for a tooth.' But I say to you, do not resist him who is evil; but whoever slaps you on your right cheek, turn to him the other also" (Matthew 5:38-39). Is Jesus abrogating the law as it is found in Exodus 21:24? Not at all! Rather, He is correcting the Pharisaical misuse of the law. This law as it was originally given served as a standard for the civil authorities in administering civil law. It was not meant to apply to individuals wishing to claim private judgment. "An eye for an eye" is not to be used as a license for revenge. The Old Testament applies the principle of "an eye for an eye" to the courtroom, "as the judges decide" (Exodus 21:22; cf. Romans 12:18f.). So then, as we read the gospels, we should expect Jesus to uphold the validity of the law as it pertains to civil government. The words of the great theologian of the last century, Robert L. Dabney, are to the point:

> The very particulars in which it is pretended Jesus amended, softened, and completed the moral law, are stated just as distinctly, although perhaps not as forcibly in all cases, by Moses and the prophets, in their expositions of the decalogue [Ten Commandments]....Christ, in His Sermon on the Mount, then, and other places, rebukes and corrects, not the law itself, nor the Old Testament interpretations of the law, but the erroneous and wicked corruptions foisted upon it by traditions and Pharisaic glosses. The moral law could not be completed [added to], because it is as perfect as God, of whose character it is the impress and transcript. It cannot be abrogated or relaxed, because it is as immutable [unchangeable] as He (Robert L. Dabney, *Lectures in Systematic Theology*, p. 357).

Christ, in His Sermon on the Mount, then, and other places, rebukes and corrects, not the law itself, nor the Old Testament interpretations of the law, but the erroneous and wicked corruptions foisted upon it by traditions and Pharisaic glosses. The moral law could not be completed [added to], because it is as perfect as God, of whose character it is the impress and transcript.

–Robert L. Dabney

Many wonder why Jesus did not say more about the individual's responsibility to civil authorities. (He said more than most people realize.) Why did Jesus not advocate the overthrow of the Roman regime? Why did Jesus not establish a system of civil government for the new Christian Church to implement in the cultures where the gospel was to be preached?

First, the primary purpose of Jesus' mission was "to seek and to save that which is lost" (Luke 19:10). There can be no godly civil government if those in authority do not have new hearts. Only the gospel can change an individual so that he will first be a self-governing individual able to govern others. Moreover, the citizens as a nation must be self-governed. Only the converting power of the gospel can bring this about. This was the starting point and major emphasis of Jesus' ministry.

Second, the gospel writers, through the inspiration of the Holy Spirit, also emphasized the gospel message and the command to obey all that Jesus had taught. Obviously this included commands that had reference to civil government. All the nations of the world were to come under the authority of the Lord Jesus Christ: "All authority has been given to Me in heaven and on earth. Go therefore and make disciples of all the nations, baptizing them in the name of the Father and the Son and the Holy Spirit, teaching them to observe all that I commanded you..." (Matthew 28:18-20). The nations were to adopt the teaching of Jesus Christ who is God.

Third, the New Testament writers proclaimed that Jesus was the King in opposition to all other kings who attempt to replace His authority with their own authority: "And on His robe and on His thigh He has a name written, KING OF KINGS, AND LORD OF LORDS" (Revelation 19:16). This statement was directed to earthly kings and kingdoms. It was a major emphasis of Jesus.

Fourth, the program for the proper administration of civil government was already part of the Old Testament message; there was no need to repeat what had already been given. Paul says, "All Scripture is inspired by God and profitable for teaching, for reproof, for correction, for training in righteousness; that the man of God may be adequate, equipped for every good work" (2 Timothy 3:16-17). These verses assure the Christian that the Bible is adequate to answer all of life's situations. This includes the area of civil government.

Fifth, when Jesus does encounter civil authorities, we can expect Him to respond in such a way as to support the validity of the law as it pertained to civil government (Matthew 5:17-19).

Do not think that I came to abolish the Law or the Prophets; I did not come to abolish, but to fulfill. For truly I say to you, until heaven and earth pass away, not the smallest letter or stroke shall pass away from the Law, until all is accomplished (Matthew 5:17-18).

Questions for Discussion

1. Evaluate the comprehensiveness of God's government by referring to the verses below.

a. Nahum 1:3; Amos 4:7

_____

_____

b. Matthew 6:26; Daniel 6:22

_____

_____

c. Daniel 4:17; Judges 6:1

_____

_____

d. Proverbs 21:1; Isaiah 44:28

_____

_____

e. Acts 2:22-24; John 19:11

_____

_____

f. Proverbs 16:33; 1 Kings 22:28, 34

_____

_____

g. Philippians 2:13

_____

_____

h. Ephesians 1:11

_____

_____

i. Isaiah 9:6

_____

_____

2. What was Jesus' response to the law and His attitude toward those who administered it? How would this apply today? (Matthew 23:2-4)

_____

_____

_____

_____

_____

_____

_____

3. What was Jesus' attitude toward those who functioned in the realm of civil government? (Luke 3:12-14)

_____

_____

_____

_____

4. What did Jesus say about the proper use of the sword? (Luke 22:47-53; Matthew 26:47-56)

_____

_____

_____

_____

_____

_____

_____

5. Is it proper for Christians to resist tyrannical governing powers? If it is proper, under what circumstances? Also, what method should be followed? (Matthew 24:15-20)

_____

_____

_____

_____

_____

_____

_____

_____

_____

_____

_____

6. What was Jesus' attitude toward the legal system set forth in Scripture and the way it was administered during His trial? (John 18:19-24 [especially v. 23]; Mark 14:53-59)

_____

_____

_____

_____

7. What status of authority did Jesus give to those who administered justice? What are the implications of such a status? (John 10:31-39 [especially vv. 34-36]; cf. Psalm 82)

_____

_____

_____

_____

_____

_____

8. What was Jesus' impression of the rulers of His day? How did the rulers see themselves? Does this mean that Jesus was against civil government? (Mark 10:42-44; Luke 22:24-25)

_____

_____

_____

_____

_____

_____

9. What did Jesus mean when He said, "Render to Caesar the things that are Caesar's, and to God the things that are God's"? (Mark 12:1-17; Matthew 22:15-22; Luke 20:20-26)

_____

_____

_____

_____

_____

a. First, what do Jesus' words say about the legitimacy of civil government?

_____

_____

_____

_____

_____

b. Second, why must citizens render ("pay back") to Caesar money in the form of taxes? (Romans 13:7)

_____

_____

_____

_____

_____

c. Third, in what way is the authority of Caesar limited? How does one determine when not to render to Caesar? (Exodus 1:15-22; 2:1-10; Joshua 2; Daniel 1, 3, 6; Acts 4-6)

_____

_____

_____

_____

_____

d. Fourth, what is Caesar's obligation? What must he render? (Psalm 2:10-12).

_____

_____

_____

_____

_____

e. Fifth, what brings about high taxes? (1 Samuel 8; Malachi 3:8-9)

_____

_____

_____

_____

_____

_____

f. Sixth, how should Christians work to overturn heavy taxation? (Malachi 3:10-12; 1 Corinthians 16:1-4; 1 Timothy 5:1-16)

_____

_____

_____

_____

_____

_____

"In this age, when [civil] government at all levels consumes an amount that is now about one-half of all personal income, it is difficult for Americans to conceive of an economy where the cost of government would be extremely low. But such is the biblical view of government according to God's design in the Old Testament economy. Until the Jews requested God to 'make us a king to judge us just like all the nations' (I Sam. 8:5), they paid *no* taxes. All social and judicial needs were ministered through payment of a tithe (which was voluntary) [in the eyes of the state] or through self-help programs in which needy people could glean the fields (see the Book of Ruth). Defense needs were apparently met by voluntary enlistment and donations of food and supplies, as shown in the example of young David's carrying food to his brothers and to the captain in the war with the Philistines (I Sam. 17:17, 18). God warned the Jews that kings would impose heavy taxes on them if they asked for a king, just as the foreign kings levied on their people. Nevertheless, they insisted that God give them a king as other nations had. Big government, then, is a pagan and non-biblical development. It is anti-Christian. Accordingly, we may also interpret as pagan and non-biblical the collection of taxes by civil authorities for government purposes beyond the limited spheres of defense and the keeping of domestic peace" (Tom Rose and Robert Metcalf, *The Coming Victory*, pp. 130-131).

10. What power legitimately was given to Pontius Pilate? In what way was Pilate's power illegitimately exercised? (John 19:10, 4)

_____

_____

_____

_____

_____

11. Of what did Jesus remind Pilate? (John 19:11)

_____

_____

_____

_____

12. What duty do citizens have when injustice is done? (Proverbs 17:15, 24:11-12; cf. John 19:12-15)

_____

_____

_____

_____

_____

_____

_____

_____

_____

_____

_____

Summary

"First, what is the final relationship to the state on the part of anyone whose base is the existence of God? How would you answer that question? You must understand that those in our present material-energy, chance oriented generation have _no reason_ to obey the state except that the state has the guns and has the patronage. This is the only reason they have for obeying the state. A material-energy, chance orientation gives no base, no reason, except force and patronage, as to why citizens should obey the state. The Christian, the God-fearing person, is not like that. The Bible tells us that God has commanded us to obey the state. But now a second question follows very quickly. Has God set up an authority in the state that is autonomous from Himself? Are we to obey the state no matter what? Are we? In this one area is indeed Man the measure of all things? And I would answer, not at all, not at all....The civil government, as all of life, stands under the Law of God. In this fallen world God has given us certain offices to protect us from the chaos which is the natural result of that fallenness. But when _any office_ commands that which is contrary to the Word of God, those who hold that office abrogate their authority and they are not to be obeyed. And that includes the State" (Francis Schaeffer, _A Christian Manifesto_, pp. 89-91).

Answers to Questions for Discussion

1. a. The natural or physical world.
   b. The animal creation.
   c. The nations.
   d. Individual men.
   e. The sinful acts of men.
   f. Chance happenings.
   g. The actions of Christians.
   h. The history of the cosmos.
   i. Isaiah makes it clear that the government rests on Jesus' shoulders. Jesus is the Governor of all creation. The government of the universe is in His hands. In Jesus "all things hold together" (Colossians 1:17). All other governments find their meaning in Jesus Christ.

2. Jesus emphasizes the validity of the Old Testament law. The people are to follow all that is prescribed in the law of Moses. "Therefore all that they tell you, do and observe" (Matthew 23:3). Anything contrary to the law is suspect. All is to be evaluated in terms of the unchanging law of God, even the character of those administering the law. Notice what happens when humanistic law is added to the law of God. The laws of men become a burden while those administering the law remain free from the load.

3. Since John the Baptist spoke for Jesus, we can assume that Jesus undoubtedly approved of his instructions. Tax gatherers should not get out of the business. Rather, they should be fair in their assessments and collections. This would apply to the civil government sending the tax gatherers out as well. Those involved in military service should not use their position of authority and power as a way of extorting favors from those under their rule. Both positions are legitimate occupations for the running of any civil government.

4. As these accounts are read, it must be kept in mind that there was only a potential threat to the disciples. While Jesus was taken away by authorities with "swords and clubs" (Jewish authorities made up of "chief priests and elders of the people" [Matthew 26:47]), it was not correct to initiate a counter-attack

108

with an act of force. Jesus had assured His disciples that He was in control of the encounter: "Do you think that I cannot appeal to My Father, and He will at once put at My disposal more than twelve legions [72,000] of angels?" (26:53). Peter cut off the ear of the high priest's servant before his own life was threatened (John 18:10). Jesus even rebukes Peter for using the sword unlawfully: "All those who take up the sword [unlawfully] shall perish by the sword [lawfully]" (Matthew 26:52; cf. Romans 13:4). In a matter such as the arrest of Jesus, the courts must decide whether a man is innocent or guilty based upon the evidence. The obligation to determine guilt or innocence is not in the hands of individual citizens. It is evident here that Jesus respects the "institutions" of civil authorities while He may not respect those who are administering.

5. Samuel Rutherford (1600-1661), author of *Lex Rex* (1644), established some guidelines for Christian resistance. Rutherford was a Scottish Presbyterian who was one of the commissioners at the Westminster Assembly in London (1643-1647). *Lex Rex* was an attack on the foundation of seventeenth century political government—"the divine right of kings"—which taught that the king or state ruled in the place of God; therefore, the king's word was law. Rutherford's work stipulated that the Law was king and that all civil rulers must obey its demands. Kings as well as subjects are under the law and not above it. When any government contradicted God's Law, that government was considered to be immoral. "It follows from Rutherford's thesis that citizens have a *moral* obligation to resist unjust and tyrannical government. While we must always be subject to the *office* of the magistrate, we are not to be subject to the *man* in that office who commands that which is contrary to the Bible" (Francis Schaeffer, *A Christian Manifesto*, p. 101).

"Rutherford suggested that there are three appropriate levels of resistance: *First*, he must defend himself by protest (in contemporary society this would most often be by legal action); *second*, he must flee if at all possible; and *third*, he may use force, if necessary, to defend himself. One should not employ force if he may save himself by flight; nor should one employ flight if he can save himself and defend himself by protest and the employment of constitutional means of redress. Rutherford illustrated this pattern of resistance from the life of David [fleeing from King Saul] as it is recorded in the Old Testament" (Francis Schaeffer, *A Christian Manifesto*, pp. 103-104).

God will judge any king who sets himself up as divine. His kingdom will be put to an end as was the kingdom of Belshazzar. Daniel informs Belshazzar of his kingdom's end by interpreting the *handwriting on the wall* (Daniel 5).

An example of petitioning tyrannical governments is found in 1 Kings 12:1-15. The people of Israel appealed to the new king, Rehoboam, to "lighten the hard service" of the former king, Solomon (v. 4). After three days of consultation with his advisers, Rehoboam ignored the advice given to him by the elders: "But he forsook the counsel of the elders which they had given him, and had consulted with the young men who grew up with him and served him" (v. 8). After hearing the king's response, the people, led by Jeroboam, fled the tyranny of Rehoboam and established a new kingdom in the north of Israel: "And it came about when all Israel heard that Jeroboam had returned, that they sent and called him to the assembly and made him king over all Israel. None but the tribe of Judah followed the house of David [Rehoboam]" (1 Kings 12:20).

Jesus established the concept of fleeing from impending trouble when He warned His disciples about the impending destruction of Jerusalem: "Therefore

110

when you see the Abomination of desolation ["Jerusalem surrounded by (Roman) armies," Luke 21:20] which was spoken of through Daniel the prophet, standing in the holy place (let the reader understand), then let those who are in Judea flee to the mountains..." (Matthew 24:15-18).

Rutherford's third recourse demands greater attention and study at this point. What method does the Christian follow to effect this third stage? Is it proper for the *individual* to rebel against governmental tyranny, or is it only proper for a lesser magistrate to rebel against a greater magistrate (e.g., a state government refusing to submit to the tyranny of the Federal government)? The instances when the *individual* may resist have already been discussed, but an appraisal of the legitimacy of general governmental tyranny in relation to the individual causes the most difficulty. When there is general governmental tyranny, the individual as an individual can only follow the first two steps, petitioning the oppressor or fleeing. When any governmental power demands that the Christian sin, it is the duty of the Christian to disobey the state's demand (see Answer 9, Third Point). The individual does not have to wait for the lesser magistrate to intervene.

But what can the individual do when there is *general* oppression by the State (e.g., oppressive taxation), and the State refuses to listen to the cries of the people and the people are not able to flee the oppression? The people then have the right to call a halt to the tyranny of the greater magistrate through the duly constituted authority of the lesser magistrate. "For a corporate body (a civil entity), when illegitimate state acts are perpetrated upon it, resistance should be under the protection of the duly constituted authorities: if possible, it should be under the rule of the lesser magistrates (local officials)" (Francis Schaeffer, *A Christian Manifesto*, p. 104). The resistance comes from a duly constituted civil authority which is joined by individual resistors. If individuals were to do it without the backing of a legitimate government, they would, in effect, be anarchists: "Anarchy is a far greater evil than the unjust punishment of individuals, because this universal disorder strips away all defense against similar unjust wrongs, both from themselves and their fellow-citizens" (Robert L. Dabney, *Discussions*, Vol. III, p. 318). Society would be in chaos if individual citizens took it upon themselves to rebel for every wrong thrust upon them.

The War of Independence is a good example of how lesser magistrates (the American colonies) first petitioned the King for redress of grievances. The original reason for the flight to the colonies was due to oppressive British rule.

When there was no response by the King to remedy the situation, the oppressed British subjects fled to the American colonies. But the long arm of English rule remained. When the long-standing oppression became unbearable, the colonies severed their ties with King George III by written declaration. The Declaration of Independence claimed that King George III violated social compacts (charters for settlement of North America granted by British monarchs) with the thirteen colonies. Within the framework of eighteenth-century English imperial government, was it "the Right of the People to alter or abolish it [British rule], and institute a new Government"? On that question, the Revolutionary War was fought. The Declaration listed "a long train of abuses and usurpations" in order to bolster the colonies' complaint against the King. The colonies, now listed as independent states, freed themselves from the tyranny of the King. Legitimate governments, the United States of America, separated themselves from an illegitimate government, English rule. "In the entire conflict from the time of the Stamp Act [1765] to the Declaration of Independence, the American position remained remarkably consistent. The colonists were defending the rights guaranteed them by their original charters at the time of emigration from England. They were not seeking the establishment of a revolutionary government. Thus, what occurred in America in 1776 was not a revolution in the normally accepted sense of the word. Actually, it was a War of Independence in which the Americans sought to preserve, not overthrow, the status quo" (J. Murray Murdoch, "1776: Revolution or War for Independence," in *The Journal of Christian Reconstruction*, Symposium on Christianity and the American Revolution, ed. Gary North, Vol. III, No. 1 [Summer, 1976], p. 87).

6. Jesus testified that He had "spoken openly to the world" (John 18:20). Since He had done "nothing in secret" (v. 20), Jesus asked where the witnesses were to accuse Him: "If I have spoken wrongly, bear witness of the wrong" (18:23; cf. Numbers 35:30; Deuteronomy 17:6). Since there was no testimony against Him (against the law), it became necessary to invent false testimony (Mark 14:55-56). Therefore, Jesus acknowledged the validity of the legal system set forth in Scripture. It is evident that corruption had so permeated the Jewish legal system that a fair trial was impossible. There were other illegalities. Jesus was tried and condemned during the night—a secret trial. A bribe was offered in order to effect an arrest (Matthew 26:14-16; cf. Exodus 18:21).

7. The passage that Jesus quotes is found in the Old Testament (Psalm 82:6). The passage refers to the judges of Israel, and the expression "gods" is applied to them because of their high and God-given office. "Jesus' point here is that the Bible calls 'gods' those who were no more than men. They were themselves the recipients of 'the word of God,' i.e. they were required to hear and heed and obey the word of God, primarily of course in connection with their calling as judges" (Leon Morris, *The Gospel According to John*, p. 527). Their actions as judges were to be identified with the work of God. The judges were to judge as God would judge; this is why the word of God is primary for every judge.

8. When rulers gain positions of power, they often seek to burden the people with the weight of their authority. In reality they should serve the people instead of oppressing those under their government. Like so many rulers in history, these rulers of Jesus' day dared to call themselves "benefactors" when actually they ruled by force and oppression. The reign of the Caesars left ample evidence. Jesus was not denouncing civil government; rather, He was opposing the abuses of those who used their position of authority as a means to exercise tyrannical power. To those who ruled justly, Jesus put forth no word of condemnation or judgment.

9. [First] Jesus does not deny that civil government has the right to exist. He acknowledges that Caesar, an evil despotic ruler, has a government that must be obeyed because all governments are instituted by God (cf. Daniel 4:17; Romans 13:1; John 18:11). This does not mean, however, that Jesus was approving of all the practices of Caesar. Moreover, citizens are not obligated to remain silent when a practice of any government is ungodly. Christians should be the first to demand that rulers everywhere acknowledge the Lordship of Jesus Christ. And Christians should be the first to change their governmental system and ways if they are out of accord with the teaching of Scripture. "We should attempt to correct and rebuild society before we advocate tearing it down or disrupting it" (Francis Schaeffer, *A Christian Manifesto*, p. 106).

[Second] Because the civil government (in this case Caesar) makes available certain benefits (e.g., roads, protection, etc.), the citizens are obligated to pay for those services. This is not to say that all the benefits that the state makes available are legitimate functions of the civil government. Many of them may not be (e.g., education, health care, welfare, etc.). However, if citizens desire these benefits, they must be willing to pay for them. It must be remembered that a gift, in the form of a sacrifice, was not being advocated by Jesus. The Greek word that is used means to "give back." Also, rulers are "due" certain things because they represent the authority of God (Romans 13:1).

[Third] "Caesar," representing civil government, can only require what is "due" him; therefore, Christians are obligated not to render to Caesar certain things forbidden in God's word. If civil authorities were to demand murder (Exodus 1:15-22); the worship of idols (Daniel 3); or the prohibition of the preaching of the gospel (Acts 4:18), it is the duty of the citizens to disobey the laws of men in obedience to the law of God (Acts 5:29). "The civil government, as all of life, stands under the Law of God. In this fallen world God has given us certain offices to protect us from the chaos which is the natural result of that fallenness. But when any office commands that which is contrary to the Word of God, those who hold that office abrogate their authority and they are not to be obeyed. And that includes the State....God has ordained the state as a *delegated authority*; it is not autonomous [a law unto itself]. The state is to be an agent of justice, to restrain evil by punishing the wrongdoer, and to protect the good in society. When it does the reverse, it has no proper authority. It is then a usurped authority and as such it becomes lawless and is tyranny" (Francis Schaeffer, *A Christian Manifesto*, pp. 90-91).

[Fourth] Caesar is duty-bound to render "to God the things that are God's" (Mark 12:17). He is not free from the obligations which all creatures have because he is a king. Rulers are in no way autonomous beings able to rule independent of God's rule. God's image is on Caesar; therefore, Caesar is obligated to acknowledge the absolute rule of God over his life: "We have, for Caesar, the image of Caesar which is impressed upon the coin, for God the image of God which is impressed on human beings. Give Caesar his money; give yourself to God....Accordingly we follow the apostle's injunction to submit to magistracies, principalities and powers, but only within the limits of discipline; that is, so long as we keep ourselves clear of idolatry" (Tertullian [A.D. 160-220]). If any ruler persists in refusing to bow his knee before his Creator he will eventually be judged and destroyed (see Daniel 4).

[Fifth] Heavy taxation is the result of two things. (1) The Israelites chose to be taxed heavily because they had forsaken God and looked to the state for salvation: "The people refused to listen to the voice of Samuel, and they said, 'No, but there shall be a king over us, that we also may be like all the nations,

114

Render to Caesar the things that are Caesar's, and to God the things that are God's (Matthew 22:21).

that our king may judge us and go out before us and fight our battles" (1 Samuel 8:19-21). The people's choice of a king was a rejection of God as their true King: "And the LORD said to Samuel, 'Listen to the voice of the people in regard to all that they say to you, for they have not rejected you, but they have rejected Me from being king over them" (1 Samuel 8:7). The people paid the price of their rejection of God as the true King. They replaced their true King with their acceptance of an earthly king to perform acts of salvation which only God can perform. Israel would be heavily taxed and turned into a slave-state where their children would be servants of the king (1 Samuel 8:10-18). (2) Failure to pay the tithe also brings judgment. God will exact his tax on His people through oppression: "Will a man rob God? Yet you are robbing Me! But you say, 'How have we robbed Thee?' In tithes and contributions. You are cursed with a curse, for you are robbing Me, the whole nation of you" (Malachi 3:8-9).

[Sixth] God has instituted the tithe as a means of financing all kingdom work. The affairs of family, school, health, the poor, and the aged are the responsibility of the people of God, not of the state. "The purpose of the tithe, in sum, is to provide the financial underpinning for the foundational work of society. As such, it finances Christian reconstruction. Society is funded and reconstructed only on the basis of the forthsetting and implementation of the Word" (James B. Jordan, "Thesis on Tithing," *Biblical Economics Today*, Vol. IV, No. 4, 1981).

10. Jesus never denied that Pilate had the authority to rule. Pilate had legitimate power to wage war against enemy nations, put down revolutionary elements within the country, and execute those judged guilty of capital crimes. Nowhere did Jesus denounce the legitimate use of these powers. But Pilate nullified his own authority to execute Jesus when he testified that he found no fault with Jesus: "Behold, I am bringing Him out to you, that you may know that I find no guilt in Him" (John 19:4). Pilate pronounced Jesus innocent. To permit Jesus to be executed was an illegitimate use of civil authority. Pilate should have released Jesus.

11. Pilate was reminded that his power was a delegated power. He did not have unlimited governing authority. His position of rule and authority was a sacred trust given by God; therefore, he was ultimately responsible to God for all his actions. Jesus assured Pilate that he was liable for his deeds. "He who delivered

They therefore cried out, "Away with Him, away with Him, crucify Him!" Pilate said to them, "Shall I crucify your King?" The chief priests answered, "We have no king but Caesar" (John 19:15).

Me up to you has the greater sin" (John 19:11). Pilate was guilty but not as guilty as the Jewish officials who turned Jesus over to Pilate. The Jewish officials should have known who Jesus was because of the testimony of Scripture. Pilate was guilty because he failed to execute justice. He crucified an innocent man: "Behold, I am bringing Him out to you, that you may know that I find no guilt in Him" (John 19:4).

12. Citizens have an obligation to cry out when an injustice is being done. To remain silent when a crime is being committed is to participate in the crime: "He who justifies the wicked, and he who condemns the righteous, both of them alike are an abomination to the LORD" (Proverbs 17:15; 18:5; Exodus 23:7). When Pilate presented Jesus before the crowd to release Him, the people proclaimed Caesar as their true king: "We have no king but Caesar" (John 19:15). The people knew that there was no damaging evidence against Jesus; therefore, they came to condemn the righteous and justify the wicked. Scripture is clear: "Deliver those who are being taken away to death, and those who are staggering to slaughter, O hold them back. If you say, 'See, we did not know this,' does He not consider it who weighs the hearts? And does He not know it who keeps your soul? And will He not render to man according to his work?" (Proverbs 24:11-12)

The first prayer in Congress, an example of the Christian heritage of the United States of America.

Lesson 7

The
Christian History
of the United States

Faith gives meaning to life. To determine the faith of a nation look to its institutions. The people, documents, institutions, educational establishments, courts, and halls of government will speak volumes regarding a nation's faith and its religious commitment. What faith did America exhibit in its earliest days? Was it a faith in the pioneering spirit? The rugged individual? A reliance upon superior reasoning? Or was our nation's faith founded upon eternal principles? Our forefathers looked beyond their own frail existence to the God who created heaven and earth. They saw the impossibility of accomplishing any task without a firm reliance upon the providence of the God of the Bible.

For generations the true story of America's faith has been obscured by those who deny the providential work of God in history. The great "Political Textbook," the Bible, has been ridiculed as an antiquated book of moral ideas that has no meaning for our day. Our forefathers, the critics say, were mistaken about the so-called absolute principles of government set forth in the Bible. A new day has dawned where the principles of the past must be cast aside to make room for the ideas of the future. Some historians even deny the Christian commitment of those who made this nation great. Modern textbooks, for the most part, delete the religious devotion of the men and women who settled this land. A deliberate attempt has been made to distort the facts of the past in order to manipulate the future. The doctrine of the so-called "separation of church and state" has been formulated on the basis of a rewriting of history. A wealth of historical evidence points to the fact that our forefathers knew nothing about an absolute separation as is being promoted by present-day court decisions.

What was the religious commitment of our forefathers, the documents they penned, and the institutions they founded? In order properly to understand the religious motivation of our forefathers it is necessary that we study the original documents themselves. B.F. Morris' monumental work, *The Christian Life and Character of the Civil Institutions of the United States* (1863), contains a staggering amount of original source material that shows the United States of America was founded as a Christian nation. This does not mean that all the men and women who settled this nation were Christians. Rather, Christian principles, laws, and virtues permeated the early colonies to such an extent that "the spirit of Christianity has entered into the foundations and elements of our national existence, and…has affected our civil and political theory, and given shape and structure to our institutions…" (p. 24). B. Sunderland, who wrote the introduction to Morris' work, said this about the Christian character of America:

> This is a Christian nation, first in name, and secondly because of the many and mighty elements of a pure Christianity which have given it character and shaped its destiny from the beginning. It is pre-eminently the land of the Bible, of the Christian Church, and of the Christian Sabbath. It is the land of the great and extensive and oft-repeated revivals of a spiritual religion,—the land of a free conscience and of free speech,—the land of noble charities and of manifold and earnest efforts for the elevation and welfare of the human race. The chief security and glory of the United States of America has been, is now, and will be forever, the prevalence and domination of the Christian Faith (p. 11).

Our Christian forefathers looked to God and His Word as they set up civil governments in North America.

This lesson will present historical documentation establishing the thesis that America was founded as a Christian nation. Our study will begin with the coming of the Pilgrims in 1620 and continue through the era of the Constitutional Convention of 1787. The page numbers are references to B.F. Morris' *The Christian Life and Character of the Civil Institutions of the United States.*

Christian Colonization of the Various Colonies

The Pilgrims who landed at Plymouth established a form of government that has come to be named the Mayflower Compact. "The form of government was instituted in the cabin of the Mayflower, before they landed on Plymouth Rock, and signed and ratified under the solemnity of prayer and the most sacred sanctions of the Christian religion: 'In the name of God, Amen. We whose names are underwritten,…having undertaken [this task], for the glory of God, and advancement of the Christian faith…'" (p. 52). "This Constitution invokes a religious sanction and the authority of God on their civil obligations; for it was no doctrine of the Puritans that civil obedience is a mere matter of expediency" (p. 52).

New England

"The synod of the New England churches met at Cambridge, Massachusetts, September 30, 1648, and defined the nature of civil government, the functions of the civil magistrate, and the duties of the citizens, as follows:

121

'I. God, the Supreme Lord and King of all the world, hath ordained civil magistrates to be under him, over the people, and for his own glory and the public good; and to this end hath armed them with the power of the sword for the defense and encouragement of them that do well, and for the punishment of evil-doers.

'II. It is lawful for Christians to accept and execute the office of magistrate when called thereunto. In the management whereof, as they ought especially to maintain piety, justice, and peace, according to the wholesome laws of the Commonwealth, so for that end they may lawfully now, under the New Testament, wage war upon just and necessary occasions.

'III. They who, upon pretence of Christian liberty, shall oppose any lawful power, or the lawful exercises of it, resist the ordinances of God,...may be called to account and proceeded against by the censure of the church and by the power of the civil magistrate.

'IV. It is the duty of the people to pray for magistrates, to honor their persons, to pay them tribute and other dues, to obey their lawful commands, and to be subject to their authority for conscience's sake.'"

"Civil government on the basis of the Bible and free principles of a pure Christianity was not the only object that the Puritans had in view in coming to the New World. They had also the great and good end of extending and establishing the kingdom of Christ, and of bringing the whole continent under the reign of Christianity and filling it with its saving blessings" (pp. 53-54).

"In 1643, a confederation between the colonies of Massachusetts, New Plymouth, Connecticut, and New Haven was formed, in which it is affirmed that 'we all came into these parts of America with the same end and aim, namely, to advance the kingdom of our Lord Jesus Christ, and to enjoy the liberties thereof with purity and peace, and for preserving and propagating the truth and liberties of the gospel'" (p. 56).

Massachusetts

"In the charter granted to Massachusetts, in 1640, by Charles I., the Colonies are enjoined by 'their good life and orderly conversation to win and invite the natives of the country to a knowledge of the only true God and Savior of mankind, and the Christian faith which, in our royal intention and adventurer's free possession, is the principal end of this plantation'" (p. 56).

122

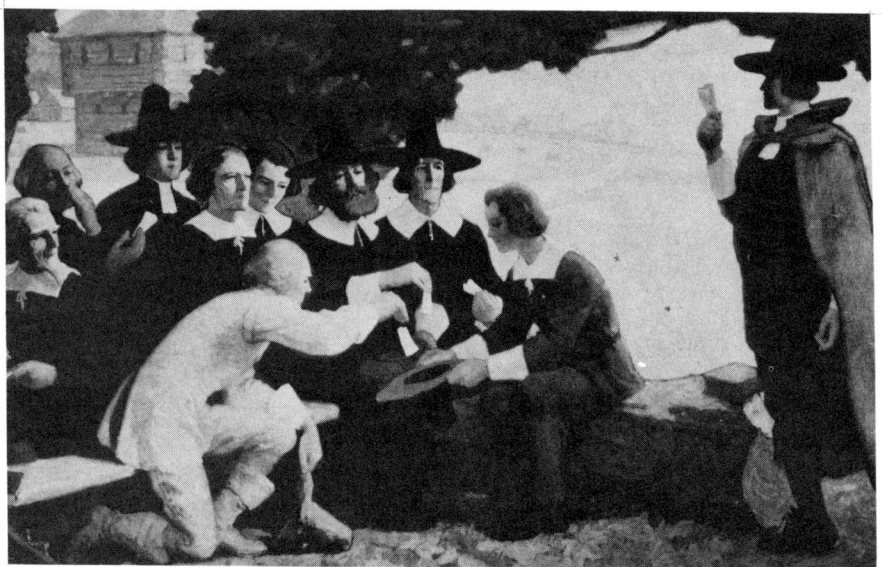

Ballots being cast for an election in early Massachusetts.

Connecticut

"In Connecticut the first organization of civil society and government was made, in 1639, at Quinipiack, now the beautiful city of New Haven...A constitution was formed, which was characterized as 'the first example of a written constitution; as a distinct organic act, constituting a government and defining its powers.'" Listed below are some of the articles which made up the constitution of Connecticut:

"I. That the Scriptures hold forth a perfect rule for the direction and government of all men in all duties which they are to perform to God and men, as well in families and commonwealths as in matters of the church.

'II. That as in matters which concerned the gathering and ordering of a church, so likewise in all public offices which concern civil order,—as the choice of magistrates and officers, making and repealing laws, dividing allotments of inheritance, and all things of like nature,—they would all be governed by those rules which the Scripture held forth to them.

'III. That all those who had desired to be received free planters had settled in the plantation with a purpose, resolution, and desire that they might be admitted into church fellowship according to Christ.

123

'IV. That all the free planters held themselves bound to establish such civil order as might best conduce to the securing of the purity and peace of the ordinance to themselves, and their posterity according to God.'

"The governor was then charged by the Rev. Mr. Davenport, in the most solemn manner, as to his duties, from Deut. i. 16, 17:—'And I charged your judges at that time, saying, Hear the causes between your brethren, and judge righteously between every man and his brother, and the stranger that is with him. Ye shall not respect persons in judgment, but ye shall hear the small as well as the great; ye shall not be afraid of the face of man; for the judgment is God's: and the cause that is too hard for you, bring it unto me, and I will hear it' (pp. 67-68). The General Court, established under this constitution, ordered,—'That God's word should be the only rule for ordering the affairs of government in this commonwealth'" (p. 68).

New Hampshire

"In 1679, NEW HAMPSHIRE, was separated from Massachusetts and organized as an independent province. The colonists, having been so long a part of the Christian commonwealth of Massachusetts, constituted their institutions on the same Christian basis. Its legislature was Christian, and the colony greatly prospered and increased in population" (p. 68).

Pennsylvania

"The settlement of the province of Pennsylvania by William Penn formed a new era in the liberties of mankind. It afforded a resting-place where the conscientious and oppressed people of Europe might repose, and enjoy the rights of civil and religious freedom which mankind had derived as an inheritance from the Creator. He [Penn] obtained from Charles II. a grant of territory that now embraces the States of Pennsylvania, New Jersey, and Delaware. He was legally inducted to the governorship of this immense domain, in England, by the officers of the crown, and in 1682 arrived in the New World and assumed the civil government of the colony. He avowed his purpose to be to institute a civil government on the basis of the Bible and to administer it in the fear of the Lord. The acquisition and government of the colony, he said, was 'so to serve the truth and the people of the Lord, that an example may be set to the nations.'

"The frame of government which Penn completed in 1682 for the government of Pennsylvania was derived from the Bible. He deduced from various passages 'the origination and descent of all human power from God; the divine right of government, and that for two ends,—first to terrify evil doers; secondly, to cherish those who do well;' so that government, he said, 'seems to me to be a part of religion itself.'—'a thing sacred in its institutions and ends.' Let men be good, and the government cannot be bad.' 'That, therefore, which makes a good constitution must keep it,—namely men of wisdom and virtue,—qualities that, because they descend not with worldly inheritance, must be carefully propagated by a virtuous education of youth' (pp. 82-83).

"The first legislative act, December, 1682, "announced the ends of a true civil government. 'Whereas the glory of Almighty God and the good of mankind is the reason and end of government, and, therefore, government in itself is a venerable ordinance of God...'" And it is the purpose of civil government to establish "laws as shall best preserve true Christian and civil liberty, in opposition to all unchristian, licentious, and unjust practices, whereby God may have his due, Caesar his due, and the people their due, from tyranny and oppression" (p. 83).

William Penn receiving the Charter of Pennsylvania from Charles II.

New York

"In 1665, the colonial legislature of New York passed the following act in reference to Christianity and its ordinances:—

"'Whereas, the public worship of God is much discredited for want of *painful* [laboring] and able ministers to instruct the people in the true religion, it is ordered that a church shall be built in each parish, capable of holding two hundred persons; that ministers of every church shall preach every Sunday, and pray for the king, queen, the Duke of York, and the royal family; and to marry persons after legal publication of license.' It was also enacted that 'Sunday is not to be profaned by travelling, by laborers, or vicious persons,' and 'church-wardens to report twice a year all misdemeanors, such as swearing, profaneness, Sabbath-breaking, drunkenness, fornication, adultery, and all such abominable sins.' These were the laws of the colony of New York until 1683" (p. 88).

New Jersey

"The high standard of Christian morality in the colony of New Jersey was indicated by the motto on the provincial seal,—'Righteousness exalteth a nation' [Proverbs 14:34]. A proclamation made by Governor Basse, in 1697, contains the following Christian record:— 'It being very necessary for the good and prosperity of this province that our principal care be, in obedience to the laws of God, to endeavor as much as in us lyeth the extirpation of all sorts of looseness and profanity, and to unite in the fear and love of God and one another,...' and 'take due care that all laws made and provided for the suppression of vice and encouraging of religion and virtue, particularly the observance of the Lord's day, be duly put into execution'" (p. 91).

The study of the history of each colony will result in the same conclusion: The Christian religion was the foundation that gave meaning, direction, and stability to the young colonies. Delaware, Virginia, Maryland, South Carolina, North Carolina, and Georgia exhibit the same religious commitment. The following lessons can be drawn from our study thus far:

"1. The faith of the Puritans, and of the founders of the various colonies, in the divine origin and authority of civil government.

"2. The subordination of civil government to the power of the Christian religion.

"3. The end and operations of civil government to propagate and subserve the Christian religion.

"4. The position and influence of the ministers of the gospel in the civil affairs of the state" (pp. 105-107).

"John Adams, in contemplating the Christian colonization of the American continent, uttered the following views of the design of Providence:—'I always consider the settlement of America with reverence and wonder, as the opening of a grand scheme and design of Providence for the illumination of the ignorant and the emancipation of the slavish part of mankind all over the earth'" (p. 109).

State Seals

| Delaware | Pennsylvania | New Jersey |

| Georgia | Connecticut | Massachusetts |

| New York | New Hampshire | Rhode Island |

The Continental Congress of 1774

"No doubt the assembly of the first Continental Congress may be regarded as the era at which the Union of these States commenced. This event took place in Philadelphia, the city distinguished by the great civil events of our early history, on the 5th of September, 1774, on which day the first Continental Congress assembled (pp. 209-210).

"The proceedings of the Assembly were introduced by religious observances and devout supplications to the throne of grace, for the inspiration of wisdom and the spirit of good counsels. The first act of the first session of the Continental Congress was to pass the following resolution:

'Tuesday, September 6, 1774. — Resolved, That the Rev. Mr. Duché be desired to open Congress to-morrow morning with prayer, at Carpenter's Hall, at nine o'clock.

'Wednesday, September 7, 1774, A.M. — Agreeable to the resolve of yesterday, the meeting was opened with prayer by the Rev. Mr. Duché.'"

Rev. Duché did pray the next morning and read from the thirty-first Psalm. John Adams, in a letter to his wife, says this about the scene: "I never saw a greater effect produced upon an audience. It seemed as if Heaven had ordained that Psalm to be read on that morning. It has had an excellent effect upon everybody here" (pp. 210-211).

The Bible in the First Congress

"The legislation of Congress on the Bible is a suggestive Christian fact, and one which evinces the faith of the statesmen of that period in its divinity, as well as their purpose to place it as the corner-stone in our republican institutions. The breaking out of the Revolution cut off the supply of 'books printed in London.' The scarcity of Bibles also came soon to be felt. Dr. PATRICK ALLISON, one of the chaplains to Congress, and other gentlemen, brought the subject before that body in a memorial, in which they urged the printing of an edition of the Scriptures" (p. 215). The committee approved the importing of 20,000 copies of the Bible. The action was taken by Congress because "the use of the Bible is so universal, and its importance so great..." (p. 216). The war had closed the shipping lanes so Bibles could not be imported from England. It was the purpose of Congress to make Bibles available to the citizens. Before the Bibles could be distributed, the war was over. Bibles could once again be procured from English printers.

"Who, in view of this fact, will call in question the assertion that this is a Bible nation? Who will charge the Government with indifference to religion, when the first Congress of the States assumed all the rights and performed all the duties of a Bible society long before such an institution had an existence?" (p. 219)

The Constitution of the United States

"[1] The Christian faith and character of the men who formed the Constitution forbid the idea that they designed not to place the Constitution and its government under the providence and protection of God and the principles of the Christian religion. [2] In all their previous state papers they had declared Christianity to be fundamental to the well-being of society and government, and in every form of official authority had stated this fact. [3] The Declaration of Independence contained a solemn 'appeal to the Supreme Judge of the world,' and expressed 'a firm reliance on the protection of Divine Providence.' [4] An article in the old [Articles of] Confederation had declared that 'it had pleased the great Governor of the world to incline the hearts of the legislatures we severally represent in Congress to approve of, and to authorize us to ratify, the said articles of confederation and perpetual union.' [5] The various States who had sent these good and great men to the convention to form a Constitution had, in all their civil charters, expressed, as States and as a people, their faith in God and the Christian religion. [6] Most of the statesmen themselves were Christian men; and the convention had for its president George Washington, who everywhere paid a public homage to the Christian religion" (p. 249).

"The Constitution itself affirms its Christian character and purpose. The seventh article declares it to be framed and adopted 'by the unanimous consent of the States, the seventeenth day of September in the year of our LORD 1787, and of the Independence of the United States of America the twelfth.' The date of the Constitution is twofold: first it is dated from the birth of our Lord Jesus Christ, and then from the birth of our independence. Any argument which might be supposed to prove that the authority of Christianity is not recognized by the people of the United States, in the first mode, would equally prove that the independence of the United States is not recognized by them in the second mode. The fact is, that the advent of Christ and the independence of the country are the two events in which, of all others, we are most interested,—the former in common with all mankind, the latter as the birth of our nation. This twofold mode, therefore, of dating so solemn an instrument was singularly appropriate and becoming" (p. 262).

The Constitution recognizes "the Christian Sabbath. *Article 1, section 7*, says, 'If any bill shall not be returned by the President within ten days (Sundays excepted) after it shall have been presented to him, the same shall be a law in like manner as if he had signed it, unless the Congress by their adjournment prevent its return, in which case it shall not be a law.'" "'In adopting this provision,' says Dr. Adams, 'it was clearly presumed by the people that the President of the United States would not employ himself in public business on Sunday.... [T]he obligation on the President to respect the observance of Sunday is greatly superior to any which could have been created by a constitutional enactment'" (pp. 264-265).

This brief survey of America's institutions and the men who framed their constitutions bears testimony to the fact that the United States of America was indeed founded as a Christian nation. The taped presentation, *America's Christian History: The Untold Story*, was produced to help the listener to appreciate fully our nation's heritage. It will present the needed background about the history of our nation and the Christian principles that were believed. After listening to the tape (35 minutes) answer the questions by referring to the Documentation pages at the end of this lesson.

Signing of the United States Constitution, 1787

Questions for Discussion

1. What was Columbus' purpose in sailing for the Indies? (See Documentation)

_____

_____

_____

2. William Bradford's intention was to lay "some good foundation." What was his ultimate purpose in doing so? (See Documentation)

_____

_____

_____

3. The Mayflower Compact was the first governing document to be applied in the New World. Why did the signers of this document undertake a voyage to unknown lands "to plant the first colony in the northern parts of Virginia?" (See Documentation)

_____

_____

_____

4. The First Charter of Virginia was a document for the new colony of Virginia. What desire did they have for the continued prosperity of the colony? (See Documentation)

_____

_____

_____

_____

5. During the development of the Constitution at the Constitutional Convention of 1787 Benjamin Franklin called the delegates to order imploring them to seek "the assistance of Heaven and its blessing on" all their deliberations. He also reminded them that "God governs in the affairs of men" and that no "empire can rise without His aid." Franklin's exhortation was heeded by the delegates, and to this day Congress is always opened with prayer. Is it possible that the delegates who were involved in the development of this nation's governing document would exclude the God who "governs in the affairs of men" from their deliberations, realizing that no "empire can rise without His aid?" How would you respond to those who say our Founding Fathers were religiously "neutral"?

_____

_____

_____

_____

_____

6. George Washington's inaugural speech acknowledged that the development of the United States seemed "to have been distinguished by some token of providential agency." What, in the words of Washington, is expected of a nation if it is to be preserved? (See Documentation)

_____

_____

_____

_____

7. What is the origin of "the eternal rules of order and right?"

_____

_____

_____

_____

_____

8. What is the implication of having eternal rules of order and right?

_____

_____

_____

_____

_____

_____

9. What conflicts do you see between Washington's words and those of our day who say Christianity should not be mixed with civil affairs?

_____

_____

_____

_____

_____

10. What duties did Abraham Lincoln espouse for individuals and nations? (See Documentation)

_____

_____

_____

_____

_____

Summary

"In 1892 the United States Supreme Court made an exhaustive study of the supposed connection between Christianity and the government of the United States. After reviewing hundreds of volumes of historical documents, the Court asserted, 'These references...add a volume of unofficial declarations to the mass of organic utterances that this is a religious people...a Christian nation.' Likewise, in 1931 Supreme Court Justice George Sutherland reviewed the 1892 decision in reference to another case and reiterated that Americans are a 'Christian people.' And in 1952 Justice William O. Douglas affirmed that 'we are a religious people and our institutions presuppose a Supreme Being'" (John W. Whitehead, _The Separation Illusion_, p. 18).

United States Supreme Court.

Answers to Questions for Discussion

1. "The Gospel must still be preached to so many lands in such a short time."

2. "For the propagating and advancing the Gospel of the kingdom of Christ."

3. "Having undertaken [this task] for the glory of God and the advancement of the Christian faith."

4. "In propagating of [the] Christian religion to such people, as yet live in darkness and miserable ignorance of the true knowledge and worship of God."

5. No, the study of America's founding documents proves that the entire nation was aware of the providential hand of God in its history. The War of Independence is a clear testimony to the fact that God causes nations to rise or fall according to His good pleasure.

6. All nations must be aware that if God is not acknowledged as the true King then there is no hope for a nation's continued existence. When a nation forgets the God who supplies the resources so that prosperity is the result then that nation can expect judgment (See Deuteronomy 8).

7. Since God is the only eternal being, it follows from this that only His rules for order and right can be eternal. George Washington acknowledged that God's laws were never-changing. "It is the duty of nations and as well as of men to own their dependence upon the overruling power of God…and to recognize the sublime truth, announced in the Holy Scriptures and proven by all history: that those nations only are blessed whose God is the Lord."

8. If there is a set of eternal rules and order then no nation can establish arbitrary laws. God's laws must be acknowledged and followed.

9. Those who say religion and politics do not mix fail to realize two essential points: (1) They fail to acknowledge the facts of history. A brief study of America's history should dispel any doubts as to its Christian character in

134

relation to civil affairs; (2) They fail to acknowledge that there is no neutral ground regarding civil affairs. Civil laws must have a beginning point of reference. Either man is the foundation, or God is. Neutrality is impossible.

10. "We ought to be...persuaded that the propitious smiles of Heaven can never be expected on a nation that disregards the eternal rules of order and right which Heaven itself has ordained."

Christopher Columbus desired to find a route to the East so he could proclaim the Gospel: *No one should fear to undertake any task in the name of the Savior, if it is just and if the intention is purely for His Holy service.*

Documentation For Lesson 7

Question 1

- From Christopher Columbus' *Book of Prophecies:*

"It was the Lord who put into my mind—I could feel His hand upon me—the fact that it would be possible to sail from here to the Indies...All who heard of my project rejected it with laughter, ridiculing me...There is no question that the inspiration was from the Holy Spirit, because he comforted me with rays of marvelous illumination from the Holy Scriptures...For the execution of the journey to the Indies I did not make use of intelligence, mathematics, or maps. It is simply the fulfillment of what Isaiah had prophesied...No one should fear to undertake any task in the name of our Savior, if it is just and if the intention is purely for His Holy service...the fact that the Gospel must still be preached to so many lands in such a short time—this is what convinces me."

Question 2

- From William Bradford's *History of Plymouth Plantation:*

"A great hope and inward zeal they had of laying some good foundation, or at least to make some way thereunto, for the propagating and advancing the Gospel of the Kingdom of Christ in those remote parts of the world; yea, though they should be but even as stepping-stones unto others for the performing of so great a work."

Question 3

- The Mayflower Compact, from William Bradford's *History of Plymouth Plantation:*

"In the name of God, Amen. We, whose names are underwritten, the loyal subjects of our dread sovereign lord King James, by the grace of God, of Great Britain, France, and Ireland, king, defender of the faith, etc., having undertaken for the glory of God and advancement of the Christian faith, and the honor of our king and country, a voyage to plant the first colony in the northern parts of Virginia; do by these presents, solemnly and mutually in the presence of God and one another, covenant and combine ourselves together into a civil body politic, for our better ordering and preservation and furtherance of the ends aforesaid; and by virtue hereof do enact, constitute and frame such just and equal laws, ordinances, acts, constitutions and offices, from time to time, as shall be thought most meet and convenient for the general good of the colony; unto which we promise all due submission and obedience. In witness whereof we have hereunto subscribed our names at Cape Cod the eleventh of November, in the reign of our sovereign lord King James of England, France and Ireland, the eighteenth and of Scotland, the fifty-fourth. Anno Domini, 1620."

Question 4

- From the "First Charter of Virginia:"

"We, greatly commending and graciously accepting of their desires for the furtherance of so noble a work, which may, by the providence of Almighty God, hereafter tend to the glory of His Divine Majesty, in propagating of Christian religion to such people, as yet live in darkness and miserable ignorance of the true knowledge and worship of God, and may in time...."

Questions 6-9

- From George Washington's "Inaugural Speech to Both Houses of Congress," April 30, 1789:

"Such being the impressions under which I have, in obedience to the public summons, repaired to the present station, it would be peculiarly improper to omit, in this first official act, my fervent supplications to that Almighty Being who rules over the universe, who presides in the councils of nations and whose providential aids can supply every human defect, that His benediction may consecrate to the liberties and happiness of the people of the United States a government instituted by themselves for these essential purposes.... No people can be bound to acknowledge and adore the

Invisible Hand which conducts the affairs of men more than the people of the United States. Every step by which they have advanced to the character of an independent nation seems to have been distinguished by some token of providential agency; and, in the important revolution just accomplished in the system of their united government, the tranquil deliberations and voluntary consent of so many distinct communities from which the event has resulted can not be compared with the means by which most governments have been established without some return of pious gratitude, along with an humble anticipation of the future blessings which the past seem to presage.... We ought to be no less persuaded that the propitious smiles of Heaven can never be expected on a nation that disregards the eternal rules of order and right which Heaven itself has ordained; and since the preservation of the sacred fire of liberty and the destiny of the republican model of government are justly considered as deeply, perhaps finally, staked on the experiment...."

Question 10

- From Abraham Lincoln's "Proclamation Appointing a National Fast Day," March 30, 1863:

"Whereas, the Senate of the United States devoutly recognizing the Supreme Authority and just Government of Almighty God in all the affairs of men and of nations, has, by a resolution, requested the President to designate and set apart a day for national prayer and humiliation:

"And whereas, it is the duty of nations as well as of men to [acknowledge] their dependence upon the overruling power of God, to confess their sins and transgressions in humble sorrow yet with assured hope that genuine repentance will lead to mercy and pardon, and to recognize the sublime truth, announced in the Holy Scriptures and proven by all history: that those nations only are blessed whose God is the Lord.

"And, insomuch as we know that, by His divine law, nations like individuals are subjected to punishments and chastisements in this world, may we not justly fear that the awful calamity of civil war, which now desolates the land may be but a punishment inflicted upon us for our presumptuous sins to the needful end of our national reformation as a whole people? We have been the recipients of the choicest bounties of Heaven. We have been preserved these many years in peace and prosperity. We have grown in numbers, wealth and power as no other nation has grown. But we have forgotten God. We have forgotten the gracious hand which has preserved us in peace, and multiplied and enriched and strengthened us; and we have vainly imagined, in the deceitfulness of our hearts, that all these blessings were produced by some superior wisdom and virtue of our own. Intoxicated with unbroken success, we have become too self-sufficient to feel the necessity of redeeming and preserving grace, too proud to pray to the God that made us!

"It behooves us then to humble ourselves before the offended Power, to confess our national sins and to pray for clemency and forgiveness.

"Now, therefore, in compliance with the request and fully concurring in the view of the Senate, I do, by this my proclamation, designate and set apart Thursday, the 30th day of April, 1863, as a day of national humiliation, fasting and prayer. And I do hereby request all the people to abstain on that day from their ordinary secular pursuits, and to unite, at their several places of public worship and their respective homes, in keeping the day holy to the Lord and devoted to the humble discharge of the religious duties proper to that solemn occasion.·

"All this being done, in sincerity and truth, let us then rest humbly in the hope authorized by the Divine teachings, that the united cry of the nation will be heard on high and answered with blessings no less than the pardon of our national sins and the restoration of our now divided and suffering country to its former happy condition of unity and peace.

"In witness whereof, I have hereunto set my hand and caused the seal of the United States to be affixed."

By the President: Abraham Lincoln

The United States Constitution

Lesson 8

The Purpose of
The United States
Constitution

Between the time of the Declaration of Independence (1776) and the United States Constitution (written 1787), the separate states operated under the Articles of Confederation (1781). These articles attempted to unite the independent states so that they could consolidate their powers in order to function more effectively, especially in time of war. The experience of war with the British, however, taught them that even under the Articles of Confederation, they were unable to perform some vital functions. "Washington's troops had gone barefooted, half-naked, hungry, and often without guns and ammunition, because there was no government strong enough to support them. For the same reason, the nation drifted into trouble after the war. Under the Articles of Confederation, the U.S. government had two fatal weaknesses: It had no power to raise money, and no power to prevent trade wars among the states—trade wars which resulted in states imposing internal tariffs, export-import duties, regulations of commerce, and the obstructions which not only clogged interstate commerce but also produced hostilities that threatened actual warfare between the states" (Lawrence Patton McDonald, *We Hold These Truths*, p. 20). In order to remedy the weakness of the Articles of Confederation, the Constitutional Convention of 1787 was called.

Because of the biblical principles that characterized the colonies from their earliest days, the Constitution reflected many scriptural principles that gave it strength and effectiveness. In order to safeguard the states from a potentially tyrannical centralized government, a separation of powers was instituted—more commonly known as the three branches of government.

What fears led our founding fathers to enact a division of powers? Their fears were, in part, historical. The experience that the colonies had with England's Parliament before the American Revolution was evidence enough that no central government should have absolute sovereign power over independent and sovereign states. The Declaration of Independence voiced the grievances of the states. The Declaration saw the expansionistic power of King George III as "a design to reduce [the colonies] under absolute Despotism" and that "the history of the present King of Great Britain is a history of repeated injuries and usurpations, all having in direct object the establishment of an absolute Tyranny over these States." Those who framed the Constitution wanted to prevent the same thing from happening to the states.

The framers of the Constitution were also aware of the biblical doctrine of the depravity of man. Man, left to his own desires, seeks to place himself in places of power and authority unless there are certain checks and balances to stop him. "When the legislative and executive powers are united in the same person or body, there can be no liberty, because apprehensions may arise lest the same monarch or senate should enact tyrannical laws, to execute them in a tyrannical manner. Were the power of judging joined with the legislative, the life and liberty of the subject would then be the legislator. Were it joined to the executive power, the judge might behave with all the violence of an oppressor" (The Federalist, No. 47).

Each state retained its sovereignty while giving the newly formed national government certain limited powers as specified in the Constitution. This was an extremely important emphasis of the Constitution. How could the states be sure that the central government would not at a later date usurp the sovereignty of the states? In order to circumvent a movement toward centralized tyranny, a system of checks and balances was instituted patterned after biblical law. "In the Hebrew republic, as in ours, there were three branches of govt: the executive, the legislative, and the judicial: ["For the LORD is our judge, the LORD is our lawgiver, the LORD is our king; He will save us"] (see Isaiah 33:22). As was the case when our nation was founded, God was acknowledged as Supreme Sovereign; His laws were law, spiritual and civil; they were the fundamental for laws and statutes enacted. Each of the 12 tribes was sovereign in its own right; the 12 were a union (one nation) under God; there was unity in God and in matters of national import; yet, no tribe or tribes could trespass on the sovereignty of the others. Within this structure and at each

142

The history of the present King of Great Britain [George III] is a history of repeated injuries and usurpations, all having in direct object the establishment of an absolute Tyranny over these States. To prove this, let Facts be submitted to a candid world.—Declaration of Independence.

level, the Lord God provided for a system of checks and balances (being aware of the sinful nature of man): the authority of the judges was checked by the senate of tribal leaders (princes); the power of the senatorial council was checked by the power of the judicial, and the people; and the whole was under the restraint and constraint of Divine Constitution, the laws of God (Deuteronomy 5:3, 27). When God permitted the people to have an earthly king, that king was required to 'write him a copy of this law in a book...and read therein all the days of his life' (Deuteronomy 17:18, 19)" (Rus Walton, "Justice and the Courts," *FAC-Sheet*, #19).

It is not enough, however, to set up a structure of national government without an underlying moral structure. The Constitution was based upon law, and that law was founded upon biblical and Natural Law (thought by most to be Christian), and English Common Law (based on biblical law and Natural Law); therefore, the values of the Constitution in general do not exist in a moral vacuum. The concept of absolute laws (both physical and moral) was believed by the majority of the colonists. Moreover, these values were promoted in and through the established institutions and elected officials and established by the Constitution and Bill of Rights. The institutions, the elected officials, and the foundational documents were to be under the "Higher Law" principles. These "Higher Law" principles would act as a barrier to implementing an arbitrary law-system. This rule of law would insure justice and liberty in a way that the whims and fancies of men would not. Moreover, both the few (minority) and the many (the majority) would be protected because the rule of law would be the standard for all. The Constitution would protect all the people—their lives, liberties and property—and avoid tyranny by one man, a minority, an established elite, or a majority.

The rule of law had also permeated the minds and hearts of the people and the framers of the Constitution were aware that they were dealing with a Christian people. It would have been impossible for them to frame a document that would not be acceptable to the Christian beliefs of the people. When the faith of the people changes, however, so does the meaning of the Constitution. As Christians divorce themselves from the realm of civil government, a moral vacuum is created that is filled by anti-Christian (humanistic) or nominally Christian government officials. So then, the Christian structure of the Constitution (a system of checks and balances) must operate with a biblical form (Christian principles of justice, liberty, peace, and law).

"To understand the American Christian Constitution as the Christian form of government, it is necessary to consider its two spheres—the spirit and the letter—the internal and the external. Both spheres must be active in order that the Constitution function to preserve the basic republican spirit of individual liberty. Today we still have the letter of the Constitution. That is, we still go through most of the legal processes of the structure of the Constitution in enacting legislation, and in the executive and judicial branches. But the spirit which was intended and understood by our Founding Fathers is missing—the Faith of our Fathers—and as our nation has fallen away from its foundations— the essence of that faith—our Constitution has become a hollow shell" (Rosalie J. Slater, *Teaching and Learning America's Christian History*, p. 240).

General George Washington In Prayer At Valley Forge.

Questions for Discussion

The Constitution

1. When you study any historical document, such as the Constitution, what things should you always keep in mind?

_____

_____

_____

_____

_____

_____

_____

2. What is the Constitution of the United States?

_____

_____

_____

_____

_____

_____

_____

3. According to the definition given in Question 2, what is the source of values and laws for a nation? What role does the Constitution play in the implementation of these values and laws?

_____

_____

_____

_____

_____

_____

_____

4. The framers of the Constitution understood the excesses of unlimited power: therefore, they divided federal power into three branches, the judicial branch, the legislative branch, and the executive branch. What biblical principles are implied in such a division of powers? (Jeremiah 17:9; Mark 7:21-23)

_____

_____

_____

_____

_____

_____

_____

The Preamble

"WE, THE PEOPLE of the United States, in order to form a more perfect union, establish justice, insure domestic tranquility, provide for the common defense, promote the general welfare, and secure the blessings of liberty to ourselves and our posterity, do ordain and establish this Constitution for the United States of America."

1. *We the People of the United States* (Exodus 15:26; 18:17-23; 19:5; Deuteronomy 1:13; 2 Samuel 16:18; 2 Kings 14:21)

_____

_____

_____

_____

_____

_____

_____

_____

_____

2. *In order to form a more perfect union* (Exodus 23:32; 34:12; Deuteronomy 7:2; Deuteronomy 9:3-7; 2 Chronicles 16:3-9; Psalm 133:1)

_____

_____

_____

_____

_____

3. *Establish justice* (Exodus 23:2, 6; Deuteronomy 16:19-20; 24:17-19; 1 Samuel 8:3; 2 Samuel 8:15; 15:4; 1 Kings 3:28; 10:9; Isaiah 1:17; Micah 6:8)

_____

_____

_____

_____

_____

4. *Insure domestic tranquility* (Romans 13:3-4; 1 Timothy 2:2)

_____

_____

_____

_____

_____

5. *Provide for the common defense* (Numbers 1:2-3; Deuteronomy 20; 2 Chronicles 26:1-15; Nehemiah 1:5-10; 2:13-20; 4:8-23; 6:16; 7:1-4; Romans 13:1-6)

_____

_____

_____

_____

_____

_____

6. *Promote the General Welfare* (Romans 13:3-4; 2 Peter 2:13-17)

_____
_____
_____
_____
_____
_____
_____
_____

7. *Secure the blessings of liberty to ourselves and our posterity* (Deuteronomy 6:24; 26:16-19; Psalm 78:5-8; John 8:36; 1 Corinthians 7:23; 2 Corinthians 3:17; Galatians 5:1; James 1:25)

_____
_____
_____
_____
_____
_____
_____
_____

8. Is the Constitution a Christian document? (2 Timothy 3:16-17; 2 Peter 1:20; Deuteronomy 10:20)

_____
_____
_____
_____
_____
_____
_____
_____

Summary

"The United States Constitution is not a source of fundamental values. It is an instrument whereby fundamental values can be protected, defining the procedures, principles, and methods whereby government can function to allow the people to give content to their lives. But the Constitution itself cannot give that content. In the early days, no one supposed that it would. There was a sufficiently clear value-consensus among Americans so that, while degrees of commitment or differences of emphasis existed, there was little doubt as to the fundamental nature of good and evil, of virtue and vice. These things were not defined in the Constitution because Americans of the federal era generally knew and agreed about what they are. Today, if there is disagreement or ignorance—as increasingly there is—fundamental values cannot be found in the Constitution. They simply are not there" (Harold O.J. Brown, *The Reconstruction of the Republic*, p. 19).

Signing of the United States Constitution, 1787.

Answers to Questions for Discussion

The Constitution

1. When you study any historical document, you should always keep three things in mind. First, you must evaluate words and ideas in the context of the era in which they were used. Words change meaning from generation to generation; therefore, it is necessary to define words in their historical context. Second, to understand properly the intent of the Constitution, you must know the intent of the writer. "If a judge can interpret the Constitution or laws to mean something obviously not intended by the original makers—then the nation's Constitution and laws are meaningless" (Lawrence Patton McDonald, *We Hold These Truths*, p. 32). Third, you must understand the historical situations that led to the development of the historical document. What led these men to direct certain prohibitions against the national government while insuring the freedoms of the individual states? There must be a history behind their fears.

2. The Constitution is a document agreed upon by independent and sovereign states to give specified powers and limitations of powers to a national governing body made up of representatives from those states. "The United States Constitution is not a source of fundamental values. It is an instrument whereby fundamental values can be protected, defining the procedures, principles, and methods whereby government can function to allow the people to give content to their lives. But the Constitution itself cannot give that content" (Harold O.J. Brown, *The Reconstruction of the Republic*, p. 19).

3. The values and laws of the United States reflect the beliefs of the people who make up the nation. If the people and the representatives they elect view themselves as the final authority in lawmaking, then the Constitution will implement man-centered (humanistic) laws. If the people and the representatives they elect see God as their judge, law-giver, and savior (Isaiah 33:22), then the Constitution will implement biblical laws and values. Thus, elected representatives will either implement the laws of God or the laws of men. There is no third way.

151

4. By dividing powers among three branches of governing authorities, the Constitution divides the potential corruption that could result if power were localized in a person (the President), an elected governing body (Congress), or a non-elected minority (Supreme Court). Moreover, no one state can influence the direction of the entire nation because its power is held in check by 49 others. The biblical doctrine of the depravity of man was instrumental in the framers' insistence of a division of power and authority.

The Preamble

1. [We the People of the United States] This language is similar to that of the Mayflower Compact of 1620, which began, "We whose names are underwritten." It is evident that the biblical concept of the covenant is implied in the Preamble of the Constitution: "If you will indeed obey My voice and keep My covenant, then you shall be My own possession among all the peoples, for all the earth is Mine…'And the people answered together and said, 'All that the LORD has spoken we will do" (Exodus 19:5, 8). Notice, however, that the elders of Israel stood before Moses as he presented to them the stipulations of the covenant. The elders represented the people (see Exodus 19:7). Elders had been chosen by the people in Exodus 18. They represented the already-existing hierarchy of the local leadership of tribes and clans that the people themselves had set up. When the Constitution of the United States was formulated, the people as a whole did not vote on it. Representatives from each of the thirteen states cast their votes on behalf of the people of their respective states. "The central government that was established by the Articles of Confederation and continued by the Constitution of 1787 was *not* established by the people acting directly either at the individual state level or as homogeneous mass throughout the original thirteen states. Rather, our general government (the national government) was the product or offspring of the compacting parties, the states, which acted as sovereign political entities and who derived their political sovereignty from the citizens. In effect and in reality, the American national government is the *creature,* and the compacting states are its *creators*" (Tom Rose, "On Reconstruction and the American Republic," in *The Journal of Christian Reconstruction*, Symposium on Politics, ed. Gary North, Vol. V, No. 1 [Summer, 1978], p. 14).

2. [In order to form a more perfect union] The idea of coming together in union (covenant) is a biblical principle if the covenant is between those adhering to the same religious (biblical) principles. At the time the Constitution was drafted, many of the individual states had constitutions that expressed their belief and trust in the God of the Bible. "If we examine the constitutions of the various States we find in them a constant recognition of religious obligations. Every constitution of every one of the forty-four States [as of 1891] contains language which either directly or by clear implication recognizes a profound reverence for religion and an assumption that its influence in all human affairs is essential to the well being of the community. This recognition may be in the preamble, such as is found in the constitution of Illinois, 1870: 'We, the people of the State of Illinois, grateful to Almighty God for the civil, political and religious liberty which He hath so long permitted us to enjoy, and looking to Him for a blessing upon our endeavors to secure and transmit the same unimpaired to succeeding generations...'" (Court Opinion: *Church of the Holy Trinity v. United States 143 U.S. 457*, [1892]). Union (covenant) among godly states, therefore, is a very scriptural principle. "Let us not estimate too lightly the theory of our government, the constitution of the United States, which has connected itself with the constitutions of the states, and made them constituent parts thereof, thus forming one system..." (Jedediah Morse, *Annals of the American Revolution*, 1824, p. 400).

3. [Establish Justice] The idea of justice as well as the idea of injustice is implied in this brief phrase. There must be a standard to determine when justice or injustice is being administered in a society. There can be no establishment of real justice unless it is biblical justice. "You shall do no injustice in judgment; you shall not be partial to the poor nor defer to the great, but you shall judge your neighbor fairly" (Leviticus 19:15). "The issue in justice is not Which one is the underdog? but Which one is right? And the standard of justice is not relative wealth or poverty, but the abiding law of God" (David Chilton, *Productive Christians in an Age of Guilt Manipulators*, p. 69). A nation which is not grounded on the God of the Bible and His law is a nation destined to reveal its basic hostility to justice. "There can be neither true order nor true law apart from justice, and justice is defined in terms of Scripture and its revelation of God's law and righteousness" (R.J. Rushdoony, *Politics of Guilt and Pity*, p. 144).

4. [Insure domestic tranquility] The purpose of the civil government of the United States is to insure civil peace within the borders of all the states. The Constitution was designed so that no state could remove the sovereign rights of another state. The ultimate purpose is to insure a peaceful domain so that the gospel can be proclaimed unhindered. Pray "for kings and all who are in authority, in order that we may lead a tranquil and quiet life in all godliness and dignity (1 Timothy 2:2). The founders feared anarchy and civil violence as well as centralism.

5. [Provide for the common defense] Under the Articles of Confederation, the states still had no power or authority to raise a militia or secure the finances necessary to protect their borders. The new Constitution would put the needed power and authority in the hands of the newly-formed national government. Through a corporate effort, the individual states would be protected. The Christian is for peace and preaches the gospel of peace, but because of the fallen nature of man, the reality of war remains.

6. [Promote the General Welfare] This is one of the most misunderstood phrases in the Constitution. It is assumed in our day that the federal government is duty-bound to provide every citizen with a certain standard of living. This is neither stated nor implied in the body of the Constitution. "General Welfare" was clearly not intended to mean aid to individuals as Madison stated in *The Federalist*, No. 41. The welfare that the Constitution promotes benefits all citizens equally (generally) and has to do with protection of the states from internal and external enemies, the financing of post offices, etc. The modern welfare system is an unequal redistribution of the wealth from one class of society to another. In reality, the modern concept of welfare is theft by law and finds no legitimacy in the Constitution of the United States. The modern concept of welfare did not become part of American policy until the 1930's as part of Franklin Roosevelt's "New Deal." "By the time F.D. Roosevelt followed in the footsteps of [Otto] Bismark [of Germany] and Lloyd George [of England], the ground had been similarly well prepared in the United States, and the use made since 1937 by the Supreme Court of the 'general welfare' clause of the Constitution naturally led to the adoption of the term 'welfare state' already in use elsewhere [e.g., Germany and England]" (Friedrich A. Hayek, *The Constitution of Liberty*, p. 502).

7. [Secure the blessings of liberty to ourselves and our posterity] True liberty is found in the lordship of Jesus Christ: "Now the Lord is the Spirit; and where the Spirit of the Lord is, there is liberty" (2 Corinthians 3:17); and, "If therefore the Son shall make you free you shall be free indeed" (John 8:36). Moreover, God has set a standard of liberty for us: "But one who looks intently at the perfect law, the law of liberty, and abides by it, not having become a forgetful hearer but an effectual doer, this man shall be blessed in what he does" (James 1:25). There is no real liberty without grace (redemption) and law (order). It has been determined that of the fifty-five men who drew up the Constitution, forty were Christians (Archie Jones, "Reclaiming the American Declaration," *Occupy!*, Vol. II, No. 8 [1980]). The writers of the Constitution acknowledge their Christian faith by declaring that liberty is a blessing. They were also aware that true liberty could be threatened in the name of liberty by a strong central government that would enslave its citizens through a system of man-made laws and religious repression. The purpose of the Constitution is to secure these liberties so that future generations will be able to enjoy what has always been protected under the Constitution. "Proclaim liberty throughout all the land, unto all the inhabitants thereof" (Leviticus 25:10). These are the words encircling the Liberty Bell. Thomas Jefferson, in 1776, wrote in his Notes on Virginia, "Can the liberties of a nation be thought secure when we have removed their only firm basis, a conviction in the minds of the people that these liberties are the gift of God?"

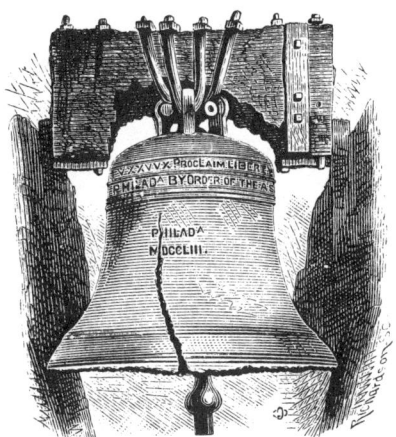

Proclaim liberty throughout all the land, unto all the inhabitants thereof (Leviticus 25:10)

8. As Christians we know that there is only one "God-breathed" (inspired) document: the Bible (2 Timothy 3:16). All other books and writings are flawed. To maintain that the Constitution is an "inspired document" (as some Mormon writers do), or that the Framers were "inspired," is heretical. The Constitution, while a literary and governmental marvel, is not inspired. The Framers were not "moved by the Holy Spirit." They did not speak "from God" as did the biblical writers (2 Peter 1:20). This means that an appeal to the Constitution is an appeal to man and is subordinate to the Bible, as is every other human writing. The Framers certainly understood this since they prepared an amendment process (*Article V*). The Bible has no amendments, nor does it need any.

Christians, therefore, should not despair if they find flaws in the Constitution. We should *expect* to find imperfections in a man-made document. The Bible is our only infallible rule of faith and practice. Such a view drives us back to the only Book where true freedom is found (John 8:36). The Constitution cannot save us. Restoring America will not come about by a greater exactitude regarding the Constitution.

William Penn, after whom the state of Pennsylvania is named, understood the relationship between godly self-government and godly civil government. The absence of godly self-government affects the whole nation through its leadership. Penn wrote, *If men will not be governed by God, then they must be governed by tyrants.*

This should not lead us to conclude that a constitutional convention is needed to revise the Constitution. Such a convention would only create more flaws since our nation's present leadership is far removed from its Christian past. We should keep in mind that the original Framers were sent to Philadelphia to *revise* the Articles of Confederation. Instead they scrapped any attempt at a revision of the Articles and created a new document. There is every reason to believe that the same would happen if a convention were called, but with sinister results. The prevailing humanistic world view would make its impression on any new document.

A great deal of debate has been generated over what the constitutional framers actually did in terms of the Christian religion. What part did the Bible play in serving as a basis for constitutional principles? There is no doubt that there is no other governmental document anywhere in the world that can be compared to our Constitution. Attempts have been made to export our Constitution, but with little success. The same religious foundation is not present in nations seeking to copy our accomplishments by using our constitutional forms.

The assumption is that since a certain type of constitutionalism works in America, then it should have an equal chance of success in any country, no matter what ideology motivates and forms the world view of the people. In essence, governmental *forms* are considered to be more important than ideology and character. This has not proved to be true. For example, "Bolivia had sixty revolts, ten constitutions, and six presidents assassinated between 1826 and 1898." Simon Bolivar (1783-1830), called the "George Washington of South America," died an "exhausted and disillusioned idealist" because of the character of the ungovernable people (Edward Coleson, "The American Revolution: Typical or Unique?," *The Journal of Christian Reconstruction*, Symposium on Christianity and the American Revolution, pp. 176-77). Some months before his death Bolivar wrote:

> There is no good faith in [Latin] America, nor among the nations of [Latin] America. Treaties are scraps of paper; constitutions, printed matter; elections, battles; freedom, anarchy; and life a torment. (Quoted in Edward Coleson, "The American Revolution: Typical or Unique?," p. 177).

When our constitutional model is sent abroad, it is then filled with the prevailing world view of the people or of the leadership seeking to create a new society. A nation going "democratic" is no guarantee that there will be any success or that the word has anything to do with the democratic process that operates in our American system. Nor should we be thrilled when we hear of nations becoming "republics." The Communist governments of former East Germany (GDR: German Democratic Republic) and the former Soviet Union (USSR: Union of Soviet Socialist Republics) used the *terminology* of America's governing principles, but in reality they are communistic, socialistic, and still anti-freedom in the biblical sense.

The success of a governing document depends on the character of the people and the world view they espouse. John Adams made this clear when he argued in 1789 that:

> We have no government armed in power capable of contending in human passions unbridled by morality and religion. Our Constitution was made only for a moral and religious people. It is wholly inadequate for the government of any other.

Where do "We the People" get this "moral and religious" instruction? Is it "natural" in man? Can morality be secured without Christ? Is there such a thing as "traditional moral values"? What was the basis of this "tradition"? Did the people of the states who ratified the Constitution in their state conventions ever imagine that the absence of any mention of God in the Constitution would affect the nation in an adverse way since the country at the end of the eighteenth century was still fundamentally Christian? Did they consider what would happen if a significant number of Christians denied their Christian calling and left the civil sphere of government? Could they have imagined that the courts would rule against the Christian religion regarding school prayer and Bible reading and would endorse homosexual rights and abortion on demand, all done in terms of constitutional freedoms, including "freedom of religion"?

We do know that, while the state constitutions began with some reference to God in their preambles, the national Constitution begins with "We the People" with *no* reference to God. How significant is this?

Patrick Henry, a Christian and a staunch believer in decentralized political power and states rights, was an early and fervent opponent of the Constitution,

The earliest civil governments in the colonies, Jamestown, Virginia, being a singular example, placed an emphasis on a biblical world view for the conducting of civil and judicial matters. Nearly every colonial government saw the Bible as a blueprint for civil reform.

as were others. He was invited but did not go to Philadelphia to participate in the drafting because, he said, "I smelt a rat." "I would rather have a King, a House of Lords and Commons than the new government," he told the Virginia state convention during its long debate over ratification of the Constitution. He would go on to give his reasons for his disapproval of the new Constitution: "Give me leave to demand, what right had they to say, 'We, the people,' instead of, 'We, the states'? States are the characteristics and the soul of a confederation. If the states be not the agents of this compact, it must be one great, consolidated national government of the people of all the States."

Under the new "consolidated" government, he warned, "other rights, too — the rights of conscience, liberty of the press, all your communities and franchises, all pretensions to human rights and privileges, are rendered insecure, if not lost." Many of Henry's fears have been realized in our day, although they were slow in coming in his day, only accelerating in the mid-nineteenth century and seemingly moving toward light speed as we near the end of the twentieth century.

James Madison, the primary architect of the Constitution, replied to Patrick Henry's question of how the "people" can institute a national government over the sovereignty of the states: "Who are the parties to the government? The people; but then not the people as composing *one great body*; but the people as composing *thirteen sovereignties*." Even so, *conceptually* the Constitution changed since the Preamble never states that "We the People" are under the jurisdiction of any sovereignty greater than the people. On paper, at least, the Constitution gives the impression that "We the People" are the voice of authority: *vox populi, vox dei*. This was a break with the past, at least in terms of the state constitutions and similar governing documents like the First Charter of Virginia (April 10, 1606), the Mayflower Compact (November 11, 1620), the Fundamental Orders of Connecticut (January 14, 1639), the New England Confederation (May 19, 1643), and the state constitutions.

James Madison, in his defense of the Constitution, wrote, in objection to Patrick Henry: *Who are the parties to the government? The people; but not the people as composing* one great body; *but the people as composing* thirteen sovereignties.

The Federal Constitution purports to be neutral toward religion. But neutrality toward religion is impossible as the Supreme Court and Congress have shown numerous times, ruling against religion in general and Christianity in particular on a consistent basis. A number of Christians during the ratification process noticed that a reference to God in the Preamble was omitted:

> Two small Presbyterian bodies, the Associated Church and the Reformed Presbyterian Church, decided to abstain from voting [to ratify the Constitution] until the Constitution was so amended as to acknowledge the sovereignty of God and the subserviency of the state to the kingdom of Christ (Quoted in R. Kemp Morton, *God in the Constitution*, p. 72).

The Mayflower Compact: *In the name of God, Amen. We, whose names are underwritten, the loyal subjects of our dread sovereign lord King James, by the grace of God.... having undertaken for the glory of God and advancement of the Christian faith....*

The state constitutions also begin with "We the people," but with a significant difference. For example, the preamble to Pennsylvania's constitution reads in part: "We, the people of Pennsylvania, grateful to Almighty God for the blessings of civil and religious liberty, and humbly invoking His guidance, do ordain and establish this Constitution." Here are some others:

Connecticut: "The People of this State . . . by the Providence of God . . . hath the sole and exclusive right of governing themselves as a free, sovereign, and independent State. . . .and forasmuch as the free fruition of such liberties and privileges as humanity, civility, and Christianity call for us, as is due to every man in his place and proportion . . . hath ever been, and will be the tranquility and stability of Churches and Commonwealth; and the denial thereof, the disturbances, if not the ruin of both."

Georgia: "We, the people of Georgia, relying upon protection and guidance of Almighty God, do ordain and establish this Constitution."

Maryland: "We, the people of the state of Maryland, grateful to Almighty God for our civil and religious liberty (declare specific rights)."

Massachusetts: "We, therefore, the people of Massachusetts, acknowledging, with grateful hearts, the goodness of the great Legislator of the universe, in affording us, in the course of His providence (an opportunity to form a compact); . . . and devoutly imploring His direction in so interesting a design, . . . (establish this Constitution)."

New York: "We, the People of the State of new York, grateful to Almighty God for our freedom, in order to secure its blessings, do establish this Constitution."

South Carolina: "We, the people of the State of South Carolina, . . . grateful for our liberties, do ordain and establish this Constitution."

162

No doubt "the people" established the civil government of the respective states (convened its legislatures and courts, drafted its laws, and wrote its constitution), but they did it acknowledging that God made it all possible and that they, "the people," were subjects and servants under His sovereign rule. This is a biblical concept. The colonial Protestant view did recognize the sovereignty of God as delegated to all civil governments *through* the people.

The Federal Constitution requires that "Senators, Representatives, . . . Members of the several State Legislatures, and all executive and judicial Officers, both of the United States and of the several States, shall be bound by Oath or Affirmation, to support this Constitution" (*Article VI, section 3*). But bound by whom? Since the constitutional covenant was made with "We the People," we must assume that "We the People" are the highest authority. In one sense they are, when the people acknowledge God as their Sovereign. But should the Constitution say more? The state constitutions certainly did:

Delaware Constitution: The following oath of office was in force until 1792: "I do profess faith in God the Father, and in Jesus Christ His only Son, and in the Holy Ghost, one God, blessed for evermore; I do acknowledge the holy scriptures of the Old and New Testaments to be given by divine inspiration."

North Carolina Constitution (until 1876): "That no person who shall deny the being of God, or the truth of the Protestant religion, or the divine authority of the Old or New Testaments, or who shall hold religious principles incompatible with the freedom and safety of the State, shall be capable of holding any office or place of trust or profit in the civil department within this State."

Maryland: "That no religious test ought ever to be required as a qualification for any office of profit or trust in this state, other than *a declaration of belief in the existence of God*" (article 37).

Because a biblical world view was still operating in the eighteenth century, presidents and other public officials as well as witnesses at trial, out of tradition and requirement by state governments, still take the required constitutional oath on an open Bible. George Washington's Bible, when he took the oath of office, was open so that on the left page there were two pictures illustrating Genesis 49:13-15, and on the right the text covered Genesis 49:13-50:8. Former President Ronald Reagan took the oath of office on the King James Bible used by his mother opened to 2 Chronicles 7:14.

The Constitution does not require that an oath be taken with the Bible in hand. But the fact that the oath is still taken in this way is a reminder that the people did not fully grasp the significance of the change in their new national Constitution (this may be due to the Christian character of their state constitutions which were still intact) or the eventual rejection of Christianity by the courts. During the time of the Constitution's drafting their elected officials still acknowledged (even the Deist Thomas Jefferson) that there is a greater Sovereign than "We the People," although this was not always understood or applied in biblical terms. It is only since our nation has become more secularized and anti-Christian that the full implications of "We the People" have come to light.

In the Bible, all oath-taking had to be done in the LORD's name (e.g., Deuteronomy 10:20). While the Constitution does not require that the oath of office be taken with a hand on an open Bible, tradition and the Christian character of the states mandated it.

In the Bible, all oath-taking had to be done in the LORD's name (e.g., Deuteronomy 10:20). The United States Constitution forbids a religious oath to be taken: "No religious Test shall ever be required as a Qualification to any Office or public Trust under the United States" (*Article VI, section 3*). This, too, was a change from the state constitutions. For example, Delaware's constitution of 1776 prohibited the "establishment of one religious sect in this State in preference to another," but disqualified clergymen from holding civil office, maintaining a jurisdictional separation of church and State, and required every public officer to take an oath professing faith in the Trinity and in the Old and New Testaments.

Luther Martin (1836-1897), delegate to the Constitutional Convention from Maryland, wrote: *In a Christian country, it would be at least decent to hold out some distinction between the professors of Christianity and downright infidelity or paganism.*

Luther Martin of Maryland, in a lengthy letter to the Speaker of the House of Delegates of Maryland set forth his justification in leaving the convention and in refusing to sign the Constitution. He wrote:

The part of the system which provides that no religious test shall ever be required as a qualification to any office or public trust under the United States was adopted by a great majority of the Convention and without much debate; however, there were some members so unfashionable as to think that a belief in the existence of a Deity and of a state of future rewards and punishments would be some security for the good conduct of our rulers, and that, in a Christian country, it would be at least decent to hold out some distinction between the professors of Christianity and downright infidelity or paganism (R. Kemp Morton, *God in the Constitution*, p. 79)

While the Constitution does not repudiate the Christian religion formally, it does seem to imply its dismissal by not acknowledging Almighty God as the source of all authority and power in civil government, the Lord Jesus Christ as the ruler of all nations, and his revealed will as the supreme law of the land. There are, however, remnants of a biblical world view present in the Constitution's covenant structure, governmental themes, acknowledgment of the Christian Sabbath, and dating. (These were pointed out earlier in this chapter.)

Moreover, the Christian religion played a significant role in the development of the nation prior to the convention and continued thereafter. So our humanist detractors are wrong when they tell us that the Constitution is *formally* opposed to religion. It is not.

George Sutherland in 1931, as an Associate Justice on the Supreme Court, reviewed an earlier decision by the Court that stated that *a volume of unofficial declarations . . .* confirm *that this is a Christian nation.* In his decision, Sutherland reaffirmed what the 1892 decision had established, that Americans are a *Christian people.*

Throughout its history our governments, national and state, have co-operated with religion and shown friendliness to it. God is invoked in the Declaration of Independence and in practically every state constitution. Sunday, the Christian Sabbath, is universally observed as a day of rest. The sessions of Congress and of the state legislatures are invariably opened with prayer, in Congress by chaplains who are employed by the Federal government. We have chaplains in our armed forces and in our penal institutions. Oaths in courts of law are administered through use of the Bible. Public officials take an oath of office ending with "so help me God." Religious institutions are tax exempt throughout the nation. Our pledge of allegiance declares that we are a nation "under God." Our national motto is "In God We Trust" and is inscribed on our currency and on some of our postage stamps (Anson Phelps Stokes and Leo Pfeffer, *Church and State in the United States*, pp. 102-03).

Acknowledging the God of the Bible as the absolute sovereign will not save our nation, but it will serve as a reminder to the people that they are but dust (Psalm 103:14). The people of Israel repeatedly covenanted before God and yet they still went after "other gods" (Judges 2:12). Their official constitution never changed, but their personal commitment did. As a nation, we need the Lordship of Jesus Christ mentioned in the Constitution, an oath whereby rulers acknowledge His lordship, and the will of the people and representatives to serve Him.

The first lesson the American Christian must learn if he would successfully develop, maintain or restore the Christian republic, is Christian self-government. Self-government without the modifier "Christian" in its full Biblical meaning, is nothing more than self-will regardless of initial intent to be or do good. Man without Christ cannot succeed in producing lasting good (Verna M. Hall, *The Christian History of the Constitution of the United States of America, Christian Self-Government With Union*, pp. II-III).

The following words inscribed on the Department of Justice Building in our nation's Capitol can serve as a summary of what we need as a nation: "Justice in the life and conduct of the state is possible only as first it resides in the hearts and souls of the citizens."

And Ezra opened the book in the sight of all the people...And Ezra blessed the Lord, the great God. And all the people answered, "Amen..." (Nehemiah 8:5,6).

Lesson 9

The Relationship
of Church and State
in the Bible

Christians have been left defenseless when they have been attacked for their involvement in the political realm. Many do not know the historical data that would give them the ammunition to answer the attacks by those who say religion should be kept out of politics. History is clear: the Founding Fathers of the United States embraced Christianity as the unofficial yet universally acknowledged religion of the land. We have seen the evidence for this in Benjamin Franklin's appeal for prayer at the Constitutional Convention of 1787, in George Washington's Inaugural speech, and in Abraham Lincoln's proclamation for "a day of national humiliation, fasting and prayer." Additional historical examples have also been given (see Lesson 7).

The study of America's history is important in understanding the context for a proper interpretation of our nation's official governing document. History records the outworking of religious ideals in a particular cultural context and gives us the record of man's obedience or disobedience to the laws of God. However, Scripture, not history, must be our final authority. "To the law and to the testimony! If they do not speak according to this word, it is because they have no dawn" (Isaiah 8:20). While Christianity's influence was pervasive throughout our nation's history, the question still remains: "What is the proper relationship between the Church and the State?" The Christian's answer should be derived from Scripture alone.

Confusion exists concerning the relationship between Church and State. Is there a biblical precedent for a separation between Church and State? If not, then what should be separated? What the First Amendment separated was the Church as an institution from the State as an institution. The First

169

Amendment's intention was never to separate religion and State. "The source of confusion comes from our tendency to employ the words 'Church' and 'religion' as synonymous. To maintain that there must be a separation between Church and State does not necessarily mean that there must be a separation between religion and State" (J. Marcellus Kik, *Church and State*, p. 124). In fact, it is impossible to separate religion from anything. Some religious or moral system is giving meaning to all laws and court decisions no matter how loudly legislators may protest that they are being "religiously neutral."

As institutions, Church and State are separate but not so separate that either one can deny the law of God as it applies to each of them. "This separation in no way implies a radical antithesis between God and State, between Christianity and State, between morality and State, between Bible and State" (Joseph C. Morecraft III, *The Keys and the Sword*, p. 2).

In this lesson, the biblical relationship between Church and State will be considered. A *functional* separation can be seen in both the Old and New Testaments. In the Bible there are clearly two separate institutions with different functions. Yet, in Scripture, both Church and State operate in terms of God's law. The separation is depicted by the use of two metaphors. The State holds the authority of the sword: "It does not bear the sword for nothing" (Romans 13:4). The Church holds the authority of the keys: "I will give you the keys of the kingdom of heaven; and whatever you shall bind on earth shall have been bound in heaven, and whatever you shall loose on earth shall have been loosed in heaven" (Matthew 16:19).

The God-given function of the Church is to carry out the Great Commission of discipling, baptizing, and educating the nations: "All authority has been given to Me in heaven and on earth. Go therefore and make disciples of all the nations, baptizing them in the name of the Father and the Son and the Holy Spirit, teaching them to observe all that I commanded you; and lo, I am with you always, even to the end of the age" (Matthew 28:18-20). The Church's task is a ministry of grace: "Therefore, we are ambassadors for Christ, as though God were entreating through us; we beg you on behalf of Christ, be reconciled to God" (2 Corinthians 5:20). The God-given function of the State is the administration of justice, i.e., the punishing of the lawless and the protection of the law-abiding: The state "is a minister of God to you for good. But if you do

Gospel preaching and teaching are essential to the Church's commission.

what is evil, be afraid; for it does not bear the sword for nothing; for it is a minister of God, an avenger who brings wrath upon the one who practices evil" (Romans 13:4; cf. 1 Timothy 2:1-2; 1 Peter 2:13-14).

The concept of a *functional* separation is rooted in the Old Testament. Moses had a special task to perform which was basically judicial in nature. He was the one who would judge between two disputants: "When [the people] have a dispute, it comes to me, and I judge between a man and his neighbor, and make known the statutes of God and His laws" (Exodus 18:16). The work of Aaron, the priest, had a different emphasis. Aaron and the priests were to govern the "religious" affairs of the nation. Only the priests could minister before the Lord: "Then you shall bring the bull before the tent of meeting, and Aaron and his sons shall lay their hands on the head of the bull" (Exodus 29:10). The "liturgical" duties were assigned to the priests (Exodus 28-29), while the judicial and civil authority resided in the elders and heads of families (1 Samuel 8:4f., 10:20f.; 2 Samuel 3:17f.).

After the period of the Babylonian captivity, the functional separation continued with Nehemiah the "governor" and Ezra the "scribe." Nehemiah was put in charge of the fortress of Jerusalem, to secure the city: "I put Hanani my brother and Hananiah the commander of the fortress, in charge of Jerusalem, for he was a faithful man and feared God more than many" (Nehemiah 7:2). "Ezra the priest brought the law before the assembly of men, women, and all who could listen with understanding..." (Nehemiah 8:2).

The New Testament maintains the functional separation. The Church is given the authority to shut the kingdom against the unrepentant, and to open the way of salvation to repentant sinners through the preaching of the gospel of Jesus Christ: "And if your brother sins, go and reprove him in private; if he listens to you, you have won your brother. But if he does not listen to you, take one or two more with you...and if he refuses to listen to them, tell it to the church; and if he refuses to listen even to the church, let him be to you as a Gentile and a tax-gatherer. Truly I say to you, whatever you shall bind on earth shall have been bound in heaven; and whatever you loose on earth shall have been loosed in heaven" (Matthew 18:15-18).

While there is a *functional* separation between Church and State found in the Bible, there is certainly no absolute separation. Both institutions have a common authority; they are both under God and accountable to His revealed word. The head of the Church is not the State. The head of the State is not the Church. Both institutions have Jesus Christ as their head. The Bible makes it clear that the dominion of Christ includes the area of civil government. He is called "the ruler of the kings of the earth." God gives this command to political authorities: "Now there, O kings, show discernment; take warning, O judges of the earth. Worship the Lord with reverence, and rejoice with trembling. Do homage to the Son, lest He become angry, and you perish in the way, for His wrath may soon be kindled" (Psalm 2:10ff.).

The Church is subject to Jesus Christ: "Christ also is the head of the church..." (Ephesians 5:24). When the church fails to respond to the claims of Christ, He is quick to exert His authority. To the church of Ephesus Jesus warns: "But I have this against you, that you have left your first love. Remember therefore from where you have fallen, and repent and do the deeds you did at first; or else I am coming to you, and will remove your lampstand out of its place—unless you repent" (Revelation 2:4-5).

172

Questions for Discussion

1. What distinctions are there between the work of Moses and the work of Aaron? (Exodus 18:13-27; 29:1f.)

---

2. In what way was there not a separation between the work of Moses (state or civil function) and the work of Aaron (church or ecclesiastical function)? (Exodus 18:20-21; Leviticus 10:8, 11; Deuteronomy 1:9-18; 17:18-20; 27:19; 31:9-13; 33:8, 10; Ezekiel 44:24)

---

3. When the time of reformation came in the kingdom of Judah, how was this separation and unity expressed? (2 Chronicles 19 [see v. 11])

---

4. During the time of restoration (post-exilic period), a separation was maintained but never exclusively. There was always a binding together on the basis of God's Word. How is this demonstrated during the time of Ezra and Nehemiah? (Nehemiah 7:1-7; 8:1-8)

---

5. There were times in the Bible when the functional separation between Church and State was denied. How did the following men who held political offices break the wall of functional separation? (1 Samuel 13:8-14; 15:9f., 21-23; 1 Kings 12:25-31; 2 Chronicles 26:16-21)

_____

_____

_____

_____

_____

6. Are Church and State to cooperate in both civil and religious affairs? Explain. (2 Chronicles 17; 19:1-11; 23:16-19)

_____

_____

_____

_____

7. Is it proper for the State to be involved in promoting godly (biblical) reform among the people? Explain. (2 Kings 22, 23)

_____

_____

_____

_____

8. Should the State involve itself in the abolition of certain vicious practices which go under the name of "religion"? (Leviticus 18:21; 20:1-5; 2 Kings 23:10)

_____

_____

_____

_____

_____

_____

9. What role should the Church take in relation to the State in offering advice and exhortation? (2 Samuel 12:1-15; Matthew 14:1-4; Acts 4:5-12; 26 [especially vv. 27-29])

_____

_____

_____

_____

_____

The Two Swords

There are two swords mentioned in the Bible. One sword belongs to the State (the iron sword), while the other sword belongs to the Church (the sword of the Spirit, the word of God). There is a proper place for both swords as we shall see, yet there is the assurance that the sword of the kingdom of Christ, the word of God, shall cause the sword of iron to be laid to rest: "And He will judge between the nations, and He will render decisions for many peoples; and they will hammer their swords into plowshares, and their spears into pruning hooks. Nation will not lift up sword against nation, and never again will they learn of war" (Isaiah 2:4; cf. Hosea 2:18; Micah 4:3).

10. What is the function of the "sword" that the Church wields? (2 Corinthians 10:4; Ephesians 6:17; Hebrews 4:12)

_____

_____

_____

_____

_____

11. What is the function of the "sword" that the State wields? (Romans 13:3-4)

_____

_____

_____

_____

12. How do the "keys" that Jesus makes available to the Church differ from the "sword" given to the State? (Matthew 16:19; Romans 13:3-4)

_____

_____

_____

_____

_____

_____

_____

_____

13. Both Church and State have limitations defined by the word of God. What limits the functions of both Church and State? (Isaiah 33:22)

_____

_____

_____

_____

_____

_____

_____

_____

14. Are there circumstances in which the Christian is to disobey the laws of the State? (Exodus 1:15-22; Daniel 3, 6; Acts 4 [especially vv. 13-22]; 5:17-32 [especially vv. 28-32])

_____

_____

_____

_____

_____

_____

_____

_____

Summary

"In summary, it is only as the church is carrying out her God-given task and as the state is carrying out its God-given task, confining themselves to what God has revealed and commanded, that our nation will know peace and prosperity under God's blessing. If the Church is not sounding forth faithfully and powerfully the word of the Lord, a nation will have no direction and guidance. If the state is not faithfully administering justice in terms of biblical law, the church will be first to suffer, when freedom begins to disappear. The only gospel that the church may administer is that revealed in the written revelation of Almighty God. The only standard of justice the state may administer is that revealed in the word of God. Both church and state are called 'ministers' in the New Testament, Romans 13:3f. A minister of the gospel does not create doctrines by fiat, he administers what God has written. So with the state as minister of God. It may not make laws by fiat. Its authority is ministerial, not legislative, i.e., its legislation and structure must be based on the laws of God" (Rev. Joseph C. Morecraft III, *The Keys and the Sword*, p. 5).

Both church and state are to operate in terms of God's commandments.

Answers to Questions for Discussion

1. It was the duty of Moses to govern *civil* affairs. He was to administer justice (Exodus 18:22, 26; cf. Romans 13:3-4). Also, he chose "able men out of all Israel" (Exodus 18:25). It was the duty of Aaron to function in the distinctly "religious" matters of the nation. As priests, the Levites were responsible for the sacrifices. Their separation was *functional* and not absolute.

2. Both were dependent upon the word of God in order properly to administer their responsibilities under God. Moses used the word of God as the standard for determining justice. The king was to "write for himself a copy of this law on a scroll in the presence of the Levitical priests" (Deuteronomy 17:18). Aaron followed the requirements of worship as prescribed by God.

3. All that pertains to the Lord (the Church) is to be handled and implemented by the priests: "Amariah the chief priest will be over you in all that pertains to the Lord." That which is to operate on the civil (State) level is in the charge of the king; "And Zebadiah the son of Ishmael, the ruler of the house of Judah, in all that pertains to the king." They were both bound by the law (2 Chronicles 19:10).

4. The Governor Nehemiah (Nehemiah 7:1-7) and the Priest Ezra (Nehemiah 8:1-8) had separate functions because their offices demanded certain specific duties as outlined in God's word. Nehemiah's job was to secure the city by appointing men who would guard the gates. Ezra was responsible for instructing the people in the word of God. Both, however, participated in the hearing of the law along with all the people, but it remained the duty and responsibility of the priests to carry out the reading and interpretation of the law for the people.

5. In each of these cases there was both a political duty and a religious duty. King Saul usurped the function of the priests by offering sacrifices (1 Samuel 13:9). The duty of the priests (the religious function) was usurped by the kings (the political function). Jeroboam, in order to save his kingdom, established a pagan center of worship contrary to the word of God (1 Kings 12:25-33). A prophet of God cried out against the king as a judgment against his evil deeds.

The king knew the law and was aware that his authority as king could not be carried over into the regulation of priestly (religious) functions (1 Kings 13:1-10). The common element was the law of God.

6. Yes, Church and State are to cooperate in both civil and religious affairs. Notice that Jehoshaphat "did not seek the Baals" (2 Chronicles 17:3). He was following the law against idolatry and "sought the God of his fathers, [and] followed His commandments…" (v. 4) Officials were sent along with some Levites for the purpose of instructing the people in the law of God (vv. 7-9). While Jehoshaphat "built fortresses" and gathered an army (vv. 12-19), it was the Levites who were in charge of teaching the law "throughout all the cities of Judah" (v. 9). Jehoiada the priest appointed the Levitical priests to their rightful position as overseers of the house of the LORD (2 Chronicles 23:18).

7. Yes, the Bible makes it clear that the State should be involved in promoting godly reform. It is the State's responsibility to displace ungodly practices that are crimes. King Josiah and the High Priest Hilkiah cooperated with one another in promoting the needed reformation of the people of Judah (2 Kings 22). The State, represented by King Josiah, had the duty to protect the Church from dangers (2 Kings 23).

8. Yes, the State should involve itself in the abolition of vicious religious practices if they are crimes as specified by God's word. The worship of Moloch was associated with the sacrifice of children in the fire: "Neither shall you give any of your offspring to offer them to Moloch…" (Leviticus 18:21; 20:2-5; 2 Kings 23:10; Jeremiah 32:35; cf. 2 Kings 17:31). The law of Moses demanded the death of anyone who offered his child to Moloch. This was a "religious" ceremony but it was to be terminated by the State. The law of God designates such ceremonies as murder; therefore, it is the State's responsibility to stop such "religious" practices.

9. The Church should perform a prophetic role in offering advice and exhortation to the State. It should remind State officials what the Bible says about civil affairs. The Church, made up of Christians, should be a voice that will encourage the State when it does right and warn and direct the State when it does evil.

10. The extension of Christ's kingdom does not advance through physical violence. Rather, "the sword of the Spirit, which is the word of God" (Ephesians 6:17) is the Christian's offensive weapon for kingdom advance. Since the nature of our warfare is spiritual (2 Corinthians 10:3), the weaponry must be of the same kind, spiritual. Spiritual weapons are scoffed at by the world, but the powers of darkness remain fearful when they are used: "Put on the full armor of God, that you may be able to stand firm against the schemes of the devil" (Ephesians 6:11f., 2 Corinthians 6:7). "The Christian is assured of victory when he uses, not the iron sword of the state, but the powerful weapons of the Spirit—in particular, the word of God" (Greg L. Bahnsen, *Theonomy in Christian Ethics*, p. 425). It is the heart that must be changed if the enemy is to lay down his iron sword. Only the sword of the Spirit, the word of God, can do such radical and complete surgery (cf. Hebrews 4:12).

11. The State functions as the bearer of the iron sword as "an avenger who brings wrath upon the one who practices evil" (Romans 13:4). Its area of authority is in the punishment of outward actions that are designated as crimes according to the word of God. God has delegated to the State the task of restraining evil deeds. The State's sword is not granted the right to enforce matters of conscience. "If one's outward behavior is within the bounds of the law [as revealed in God's Word] he has nothing to fear from the civil magistrate—even if he is an idolator, murderer, or whatever in his heart" (Greg L. Bahnsen, *Theonomy in Christian Ethics*, p. 427). [Lesson Four, Answer 10 (NOTE) discusses the difference between a sin and a crime.]

12. The Church, the body of Christ, is in possession of the keys of the kingdom. It is the Church's responsibility to make the way of life open to those who are outside the kingdom. "First, he [Jesus] says that the ministers of the Gospel are porters, so to speak, of the kingdom of heaven, because they carry its keys; and, secondly, he adds, that they are invested with a power of binding and loosing, which is ratified in heaven. The comparison of the keys is very properly applied to the office of teaching; as when Christ says (Luke xi. 52) that the scribes and Pharisees, in like manner, have the key of the kingdom of heaven, because they are expounders of the law ["Woe to you lawyers! For you have taken away the key of knowledge; you did not enter in yourselves, and those who were entering in you hindered."]. We know that there is no other way in which the gate of life is opened to us than by the word of God [the sword of the Spirit]; and hence it follows that the key is placed, as it were, in the hands of the ministers of the word" (John Calvin, *Commentary on a Harmony of the Evangelists, Matthew, Mark, and Luke*, Vol. II, p. 292). The jurisdiction of the State lies outside the realm of the keys. The State is to be faithful to the word of God but its area of operation is the judicial realm. It is to concern itself with crimes as specified by the word of God. It should not overstep its bounds to dictate to the Church its proper administration of the keys.

13. Scripture is clear: "For the Lord is our judge, the Lord is our lawgiver, the Lord is our king; He will save us" (Isaiah 33:22). The institutions of the Church and State must operate in the context of God's law-word as the standard. Neither institution can overstep its bounds of authority without violating the word of God. The rule of God is authoritative in the Church as well as in the State. Jesus is seated above every rule and authority. Finally, salvation cannot be secured by either institution. The person and work of Jesus Christ saves. There is salvation in no other name (Acts 4:12).

14. (1) Only if those laws are in direct opposition to biblical commands. If the State commands murder then we must disobey the state. (2) State or emperor worship is to be repudiated. No Christian is ever to forsake the worship of the true God no matter how great the penalty. (3) The command to preach the gospel (Matthew 28:18-20) overrules the command of the civil authorities to stop preaching the gospel. [A fuller discussion of this question was presented in Lesson Six.]

The early church rejected Caesar Worship.

181

Solomon's prayer for wisdom should remind all civil leaders that there is a proper biblical and constitutional bala
between church and civil relationships. We see more civil intrusion into religion the more rulers reject the wisc
that only comes from God through His Word.

Lesson 10

The Relationship of Church and State in the First Amendment

There is great confusion in our day—among Christians as well as non-Christians—regarding the relationship of Church and State. Christians have bought the idea that "religion" is not to be part of any political system. They are so sure of this that they point to the First Amendment of the Constitution for their ideological support. They are confident that it requires a "separation between Church and State" and that biblical principles must not be brought to bear on social and political issues.

This lesson attempts to dispel currently-held misconceptions regarding Church/State relations concerning the so-called "separation of Church and State," misconceptions that have been taught over the years and that now have come to be regarded as fact. These misconceptions are myths. To accept these myths of an *absolute* separation of Church and State is to accept the separation of God from civil government. Such myths lead to the judgment of God and national destruction. In a "Sermon on National Sins," James H. Thornwell addressed the idea of separating Christianity from the State. Even though the sermon was preached more than 100 years ago, it is more applicable today than when it was first given:

> When we insist upon the religious character of the State, we are not to be understood as recommending or favouring a Church Establishment. To have a religion is one thing, to have a Church Establishment is another; and perhaps the most effectual way of extinguishing the religious life of a State is to confine the expression of it to the forms and peculiarities of a single sect [denomination]. The Church and State, as

visible institutions, are entirely distinct, and neither can usurp the province of the other without injury to both. But religion, as a life, as an inward principle, though specially developed and fostered by the Church, extends its domain beyond the sphere of technical worship, touches all the relations of man, and constitutes the inspiration of every duty. The service of the Commonwealth becomes an act of piety to God. The State realizes its religious character through the religious character of its subjects; and a State is and ought to be Christian, because all its subjects are and ought to be determined by the principles of the Gospel. As every legislator is bound to be a Christian man, he has no right to vote for any laws which are inconsistent with the teachings of Scriptures. He must carry his Christian conscience into the halls of legislation *(The Collected Writings of James Henley Thornwell*, Vol. IV, p. 517).

The first myth which most people believe is that a system of law and its principles somehow can be religiously or morally neutral. It must be remembered, however, that neutrality is impossible. Some authority, whether it be God or man, is used as the reference point for all enacted laws. If a political system rejects one authority, it adopts another. If a biblical moral system is not being legislated, then an immoral system is being legislated. Any moral system

Our standard of right is that eternal law which God proclaimed from Sinai, and which Jesus expounded on the Mount. We recognize our responsibility to Jesus Christ. He is Head over all things to the Church, and the nation that will not serve Him is doomed to perish.

–James Henley Thornwell

that does not put Jesus Christ at its center, denies Christ: "No one can serve two masters; for either he will hate the one and love the other, or he will hold to one and despise the other..." (Matthew 6:24); and, "He who is not with Me is against Me; and he who does not gather with Me scatters" (12:30). "Our standard of right is that eternal law which God proclaimed from Sinai, and which Jesus expounded on the Mount. We recognize our responsibility to Jesus

Christ. He is Head over all things to the Church, and the nation that will not serve Him is doomed to perish" (James Henley Thornwell, *The Collected Writings of James Henley Thornwell*, Vol. IV, p. 517f.).

The second myth is that the First Amendment calls for a "separation of Church and State." When an individual is questioned as to whether a Christian should involve himself in the political realm, a protest is made by an appeal to the "separation of Church and State" found in the First Amendment to the Constitution. Many Christians usually do not have an answer when they are confronted with this standard argument. Most people do not realize that the First Amendment says nothing about Church and State or a separation between the two. It simply states that "Congress shall make no law respecting an establishment of religion, or prohibiting the free exercise thereof...." In the Constitution of the Soviet Union, however, the doctrine of the separation of Church and State is found: "In order to ensure to citizens freedom of conscience, the church in the U.S.S.R. is separated from the State, and the school from the church. Freedom of religious worship and freedom of anti-religious propaganda is recognized for all citizens" (*Article 124*). The Constitution of the United States of America has the First Amendment as a safe-guard so that the State can have no jurisdiction over the Church. Its purpose was to protect the Church not to disestablish it.

The third myth concerns the silence of the Constitution regarding Christianity. It is assumed that the United States was never Christian in its basic ideals and values because the Constitution does not specifically mention Christianity. The myth is shattered when one realizes that it was never the purpose of the Constitution to give religious content to the nation. Rather, the Constitution was an instrument whereby already existing religious values of the nation could be protected and perpetuated. The Constitution is not devoid of Christian references, however. It is interesting to note that the Constitution acknowledges Sunday as a day of rest: "If any bill shall not be returned by the President within ten days (Sundays excepted) after it shall have been presented to him, the same shall be a law..." (*Article I, section 7*). Moreover, there is a direct reference to the Lord Jesus Christ in the Constitution: "DONE in convention by the unanimous consent of the States present, the seventeenth of September, in the year of our Lord one thousand seven hundred and eighty seven and of the independence of the United States of America the twelfth. In witness whereof we have hereunto subscribed our Names."

The fourth myth is a belief that the states were to be religiously neutral and that the federal government had an obligation to ensure that the states remained religiously neutral. By studying the State Constitutions, one begins to realize that they were not religiously "neutral" but were, in fact, explicitly Christian. After the adoption of the First Amendment, several states even had established Churches. Here are some examples:

The Connecticut Constitution (until 1818): "The People of this State...by the Providence of God...hath the sole and exclusive right of governing themselves as a free, sovereign, and independent State...and forasmuch as the free fruition of such liberties and privileges as humanity, civility, and Christianity call for, as is due to every man in his place and proportion...hath ever been, and will be the tranquility and stability of Churches and Commonwealth; and the denial thereof, the disturbances, if not the ruin of both."

The Delaware Constitution (1831): "...no man ought to be compelled to attend any religious worship..." but it recognized "the duty of all men frequently to assemble together for the public worship of the Author of the Universe." The following oath of office was in force until 1792: "I...do profess faith in God the Father, and in Jesus Christ His only son, and in the Holy Ghost, one God, blessed for evermore; I do acknowledge the holy scriptures of the Old and New Testaments to be given by divine inspiration."

The Maryland Constitution (until 1851): "That, as it is the duty of every man to worship God in such a manner as he thinks most acceptable to him; all persons professing the Christian religion, are equally entitled to protection in their religious liberty; wherefore no person ought by any law to be molested...on account of his religious practice; unless, under the color [pretense] of religion, any man shall disturb the good order, peace or safety of the State, or shall infringe the laws of morality...yet the Legislature may, in their discretion, lay a general and equal tax, for the support of the Christian religion." The Constitution of 1864 required "a declaration of a belief in the Christian religion" for all State officers.

The Massachusetts Constitution (until 1863): This state Constitution included the "right" of "the people of this commonwealth to...invest their Legislature with power to authorize and require, the several towns, parishes, precincts, and other bodies-politic or religious societies to make suitable provision, at their own expense, for the institution of the public worship of God and for the support and maintenance of public Protestant teachers of piety, religion, and morality in all cases where such provision shall not be made voluntary."

The North Carolina Constitution (until 1876): "That no person who shall deny the being of God, or the truth of the Protestant religion, or the divine authority of the Old or New Testaments, or who shall hold religious principles incompatible with the freedom and safety of the State, shall be capable of holding any office or place of trust or profit in the civil department within this State."

These State Constitutions provide ample evidence that the First Amendment was not originally intended to remove all Christian influence from our civil government. "And yet, the Supreme Court and some Constitutional authorities ask us to believe that the founding fathers would have forbidden even a voluntary prayer in a school supported by a State....Paul Eidelberg (*The Philosophy of the American Constitution*, p. 271), having cited these provisions of the State constitutions, remarks that the various decisions of the Supreme Court regarding the First Amendment and the 'establishment of religion' clause should be reviewed in the light of this information" (James M. Bulman, *It Is Their Right*, pp. 111-112, 119).

The fifth myth that has permeated our thinking is that historically the concept of the separation of Church and State has been part of official governmental policy. "If the American people have ever adopted the principle of complete separation of church and state, we would find the evidence of it in the federal Constitution, in the acts of Congress, or in the constitutions or laws of the several states. There is no such evidence in existence. In its absence, the mere opinion of private individuals or groups that there should be absolute separation of church and state (a condition that has not existed in recent centuries in any civilized nation on earth) does not create a 'great American principle'" (J.M. O'Neill, *Religion and Education Under the Constitution*, p. 4). The origin of the phrase "separation of church and state" is found in a letter from Thomas Jefferson to a group of Baptist clergymen (January 1, 1802). Jefferson was assuring the Danbury Baptist Association that the First Amendment guaranteed that there would be no establishment of any one denomination over another. The Baptists feared that the Congregationalists would be the preferred denomination. The Supreme Court has taken Jefferson's "separation" clause (divorced from Jefferson's own explanation of the phrase) and used it to create a new, and completely arbitrary, interpretation of the First Amendment.

Since Jefferson is the best interpreter of Jefferson, his own words concerning the issue of the national government's authority over individual states and churches should be considered. In Jefferson's Second Inaugural Address of March 4, 1805, he made the following comment: "In matters of religion, I have considered that its free exercise is placed by the Constitution independent of the powers of the General Government. I have therefore undertaken, on no occasion, to prescribe the religious exercise suited to it; but have left them, as the Constitution found them, under the direction and discipline of state and church authorities acknowledged by the several religious societies" (Saul K. Padover, ed., *The Complete Jefferson*, p. 412).

Jefferson feared the Supreme Court. He believed that the Court by tis exercise of the power of judicial review was in the process of usurping the authority of the national and state governments. In 1820 he wrote: "To consider the judges as the ultimate arbiters of all constitutional questions is a very dangerous doctrine indeed, and one which would place us under the despotism of an oligarch [rule by a few]. . . . The Constitution has erected no such single tribunal, knowing that to whatever hands confided, with the corruptions of time and party, its members would become despots" (Letter to William Charles Jarvis, 1820).

Jefferson did not deny the validity of judicial review of congressional actions as they related to the rights of individuals. Rather, he was against the groundless presumption of authority over the executive and legislative branches of the federal government. The judiciary was equally bound by the Constitution; the court ought not to rule independent of it.

But a most fundamental question remains: What is the proper relationship between religion and civil government as it is described in the First Amendment?

Questions for Discussion

The First Amendment

1. "Congress shall make no law respecting an establishment of religion, or prohibiting the free exercise thereof...." What two prohibitions are listed?

_____

_____

_____

_____

_____

2. To whom are the prohibitions addressed?

_____

_____

_____

_____

_____

3. Why was a Bill of Rights added to the Constitution in 1791?

_____

_____

_____

_____

_____

4. What is the history behind the "establishment of religion" clause? Why was the clergy so insistent that this clause be included?

_____

_____

_____

_____

_____

_____

5. Does the First Amendment require the federal government to be secularized, devoid of any religious considerations that are Christian?

_____
_____
_____
_____
_____
_____

6. Since the First Amendment does not mention the Christian religion specifically, can we then assume that this amendment was hostile to Christianity? Explain. Does the Constitution mention the Christian religion indirectly? Where?

_____
_____
_____
_____
_____

7. Where did the concept of "the separation of Church and State" originate? What was the purpose of stating that there was a separation between Church and State?

_____
_____
_____
_____
_____
_____

8. Is Jefferson's concept of separation implied in the First Amendment?

_____
_____
_____
_____
_____

9. How did Jefferson clarify his 1802 declaration?

_____

_____

_____

_____

10. What does the First Amendment mean for us today?

_____

_____

_____

_____

11. Since the time of the drafting of the Constitution and the Bill of Rights, what has happened to the application of the Bill of Rights in reference to the states?

_____

_____

_____

_____

12. How did the Fourteenth Amendment reverse the application of the Bill of Rights, especially the First Amendment, so that it now applies to the states?

_____

_____

_____

_____

_____

13. What was the prayer that was said in public schools that brought about the prayer ban of 1962? How have the courts been able to make their misrepresentation of the First Amendment apply to education?

_____

_____

_____

_____

_____

Summary

"At his inaugural ceremony, the President of the United States is given the oath of office; with right hand on the holy Bible, the President avows, 'I solemnly swear to support and defend the Constitution of the United States.' What is tragic is that many Presidents have made a solemn oath on the Word of the sovereign God they know nothing about. Those who strive to isolate religion completely from government, business, and education are in reality attempting to destroy the Christian religion. While trying to make this country free from religion, they are destroying the nation. There is no reason the government and the Christian religion cannot cooperate and work together. This is the American tradition that was intended to be protected by the First Amendment" (John W. Whitehead, *The Separation Illusion*, p. 123).

George Washington takes the oath of office as President of the United States with his hand on an open Bible where two pictures illustrate the events depicted in Genesis 49:13-50:8.

Answers to Questions for Discussion

1. First, no law is to be made that would establish one religious denomination over any other religious denomination. That this is the intent of the amendment is made clear by other proposed amendments: "Congress shall make no law establishing one Religious Sect or Society in preference to others, or prohibiting the free exercise thereof, nor shall the rights of conscience be infringed." Another text was as follows: "Congress shall make no law establishing any particular denomination of religion in preference to another, or prohibiting the free exercise thereof, nor shall the rights of conscience be infringed." The reason that these amendments were not adopted is because they did not offer enough protection for the individual states. The framers of the First Amendment wanted to be assured that the Federal government would not involve itself in any religious practice. Second, no law is to be made which would prohibit anyone from fully exercising his or her religious beliefs.

2. The prohibition is addressed to Congress since Congress is the only national law-making body of civil government. Congress, therefore, is prohibited from either establishing a national religion or denying any state, institution, or individual the freedom of determining its religious affairs.

3. A Bill of Rights was added to the Constitution in 1791 because many people believed that the Constitution was not specific enough regarding the rights of the states and the people. The individual states felt that a Bill of Rights "would protect fundamental rights against interference by the new federal government" (John W. Whitehead, *The Separation Illusion*, p. 68). The purpose of the Bill of Rights, therefore, was to restrict the federal government from exercising its power in certain areas. In the case of the First Amendment, the power of Congress was limited in the areas of religion, free speech, and assembly.

4. The establishment clause was a protection that the leaders in the states wanted so that they would not suffer the same religious persecutions that their forefathers had experienced. It was imperative that the newly-formed powers of the federal government could not be used to force a certain national religious denomination on any people or infringe on religious affairs of any kind. The people then would be free to live out their religious convictions in peace without interference from Congress. "It would not have occurred to them [representatives from the states] to attempt to re-establish that which the colonists had fought against, namely, religious control and establishment by the central government" (R.J. Rushdoony, *The Nature of the American System*, p. 3).

5. The First Amendment does not require the federal government to be secularized. The early history of the United States, both before and after ratification of the Bill of Rights, shows that no secularization took place. Congress began its sessions with divine worship. After the adoption of the First Amendment, the federal government reenacted the policy of the Northwest Ordinance by declaring: "Religion, morality, and knowledge being necessary to good government and the happiness of mankind, schools and the means of education shall forever be encouraged." Moreover, national days of prayer and fasting were instituted by most of our presidents and are continued to this day.

6. The fact that Christianity is not specifically mentioned does not mean that the First Amendment is hostile to Christianity. The First Amendment was intended to limit Congress in its use of power regarding religion, including the Christian religion. The only authority that the federal government has is specified in the Constitution. "Since Christianity was not mentioned in the Constitution, the federal government had no control over it" (John W. Whitehead, *The Separation Illusion*, p. 24). As was pointed out in the introduction, the Constitution does contain references to Christianity. Sunday as a day of rest (*Article 1, section 7*) and a direct reference to the Lord Jesus Christ, "this done in the year of our LORD," are part of the Constitution. The framers of the Constitution did not seek to establish a new calendar with a new year one.

7. The phrase "a wall of separation between Church and State" had its origin in a letter written by Thomas Jefferson in 1802 to a group of Baptists in Danbury, Connecticut. Jefferson's purpose was to assure the Baptists that no national church [Congregational in this instance] would be adopted. Should a letter of a president to a group of churchmen become public policy? This is what has happened. Our courts have substituted Thomas Jefferson's misunderstood phrase for the true meaning of the First Amendment.

8. It must be remembered that Thomas Jefferson did not have a hand in the drafting of the Constitution or the First Amendment. In fact, Jefferson was in Paris in 1791 when the First Amendment was written. The idea of such a total separation, as used today, is an interpretation not based upon the language of the amendment or the historical context in which it was written. Consider these words by Thomas Jefferson: "I consider the government of the United States as interdicted [prohibited] by the Constitution from intermeddling with religious institutions, their doctrines, discipline, or exercises. This results not only from the provision that no law shall be made respecting an establishment or free exercise of religion, but from that also which reserves to the states the powers not delegated to the general government. It must then rest with the states, as far as it can be in any human authority..." (Letter to Samuel Miller, January 23, 1808).

9. Jefferson clarified his 1802 concept of the First Amendment during his Second Inaugural Address, 1805, when he stated, "In matters of religion I have considered that its free exercise is placed by the Constitution independent of the powers of the General [federal] Government. I have therefore undertaken on no occasion to prescribe the religious exercises suited to it, but have left them, as the Constitution found them, under the direction and discipline of the church or state authorities acknowledged by the several religious societies."

10. Historically understood, the First Amendment would read: "The federal government shall make no law having anything to do with supporting a single church, or government preference of one Christian creed or denomination over another....The First Amendment, therefore, provides freedom for religion, not from religion. The states by this amendment were afforded that freedom in the area of religion" (John W. Whitehead, *The Separation Illusion*, pp. 90-91).

11. The original purpose of the Bill of Rights was to restrict the federal government's power over the states; it was to protect the "rights" of the states. After the War Between the States the Fourteenth Amendment (1868) was added to the Constitution. Subsequent interpretations of this amendment applied the prohibitions of the Bill of Rights against the states as well as against the federal government. This was a reversal of their original purpose. Now the states are without the freedoms granted to them in the Bill of Rights. As a result of this high-handed undermining of states' rights, the Federal Government's authority and power are unrestrained and unlimited. "The application, in any manner, of the establishment of religion clause of the First Amendment to the legislatures of the several states was unpremeditated, unforeseen, unintended by the men responsible for the Fourteenth Amendment. The application to the states of the Congressional restrictions mentioned in any part of the First Amendment was not 'assumed' by the Supreme court until fifty-seven years after the ratification of the Fourteenth [In *New York v. Gitlow*, 268 U.S. 652 (1925)]. So far as the relation of government to an establishment of religion is concerned, any influence that is now or ever will be exercised by the Fourteenth Amendment, is a clear constitutional accident" (J.M. O'Neill, *Religion and Education Under the Constitution*, p. 155).

12. In *Engel v. Vitale* (1962), Justice Hugo Black stated that "the constitutional prohibition against laws respecting an establishment of religion must at least mean that in this country it is not part of the business of government to compose official prayers for any group of the American people to recite as part of a religious program carried on by government." Justice Black's declaration made it clear "that the public domain is out of bounds for God" (John W. Whitehead, *The Separation Illusion*, p. 108). Justice Black ignored over 300 years of American history in the process. This trend toward complete secularization was extended when the Supreme Court struck down Bible reading as part of the daily devotional life of the public schools.

13. "Almighty God, we acknowledge our dependence upon thee, and we beg thy blessings upon us, our parents, our teachers, and our country." How could Lincoln proclaim a national day of prayer and that not be an establishment of religion while a twenty-two word prayer written by the New York State Board of Regents is? Remember, the Bill of Rights is a restriction on Congress, not the states. It should be kept in mind that education is not a domain of control for the federal government. At the time of the drafting of the Constitution and the Bill of Rights there was no Department of Education. Since that time, however, education has come increasingly under the jurisdiction of the Federal Government. Any attempt to do anything "religious" in tax-supported schools is prohibited by the Federal government because it is interpreted as an establishment of religion.

All Scripture is inspired by God and profitable for teaching, for reproof, for correction, for training in righteousness; that the man of God may be adequate, equipped for every good work (2 Timothy 3:16-17).

What is Government?

Government consists of **sovereignty** (legitimacy to rule: Romans 13:1), **representation** (accountability to the rule of another: Exodus 18:17-23), **law** (a moral code by which to rule: Romans 13:4), **jurisdiction** (authority to enforce sanctions in the name of the ruler: 1 Peter 2:13-14), and **continuity** (stability and longevity of government: Deuteronomy 28).

1. Sovereignty: Legitimacy to Rule

The Apostle Paul writes that "all authority comes from God" (Romans 13:1) because only God is absolutely sovereign and omnipotent (1 Timothy 6:15-16; Revelation 4:8, 11). Rulers, therefore, only have *limited* authority to govern. God delegates this limited sovereignty to every government (family, church, and civil).

Nebuchadnezzar, ruler in Babylon and claimant of absolute and unlimited sovereignty, recognized the delegated nature of his governmental sovereignty when God made his "dwelling place with the beasts of the field" (Daniel 4:30-33). After being treated like an animal with no sovereignty (Genesis 2:18-20), Nebuchadnezzar repented affirming that God's "dominion is an everlasting dominion, and His kingdom endures from generation to generation" (Daniel 4:34). It was after this that he was reinstalled to his rightful limited sovereignty *under* God's absolute government: "My majesty and splendor were *restored* to me for the glory of my kingdom, and my counselors and my nobles began seeking me out; so I was *reestablished* in my sovereignty, and surpassing greatness was added to me" (v. 4:36). To be *restored* and *reestablished* assumes an initial installation and establishment.

Having sovereignty to govern does not mean that rulers, whether they are fathers and mothers in family government, elders in church government, or civil servants in civil government, always exercise their authority legitimately. It only means that the government is legitimate and must be obeyed unless there is *biblical* cause for disobedience.

The biblical philosophy of sovereignty and legitimacy in government explains why rebellion against duly constituted governments (family, church, and civil) is sin (Exodus 22:28; Acts 23:5). "For rebellion is as the sin of divination, and insubordination is as iniquity and idolatry" (1 Samuel 15:23).

Governments that are formed are legitimate even though they may not be acting in a legitimate way. Who would determine when a government has overstepped the boundary of legitimacy? No earthly government is perfect. As Christians, we do not believe in the possibility of utopianism this side of heaven. When David was being pursued by King Saul, David had the opportunity to take the king's life. He could have claimed that he was doing it for "the people." He did not.

> Behold, this day your eyes have seen that the LORD had given you today into my hand in the cave, and some said to kill you, but my eye had pity on you; and I said, "I will not stretch out my hand against my lord, *for he is the LORD's anointed*" (1 Samuel 24:10).

Legitimacy in government is essential if any nation is to endure. If people perceive that their government lacks legitimacy, anarchy and revolution will result. Our world is filled with folk who believe that the citizenry have a right to revolt against an oppressive government even though those in power claim their regime to be legitimate. King Saul was an oppressor, but David saw no justification in killing him, even when he had the opportunity (vv. 11-14). God will be the one to deliver the oppressed from the hand of the oppressors: "The LORD therefore be judge between you and me; and may He see and plead my cause, and deliver me from your hand" (v. 15). Deliverance is to come God's way.

Wherever Christians find themselves under the rule of a tyrant, they are to live under it, but not with resignation (Luke 20:19-25; 1 Timothy 2:1-3; Titus 3:1; 1 Peter 2:13-17). God has made non-revolutionary means available for the dissolution of tyrannical governments. In addition, God providentially works to overrule the works of men. Man proposes, but God disposes. "The king's heart is like channels of water in the hand of the LORD; He turns it wherever He wishes" (Proverbs 21:1).

2. Representation: Accountability to the Rule of Another

All governments **represent** (accountability to the rule of another) the sovereignty of a superior; that is, no single earthly government can claim to be *the* government independent either of God or other governments. In addition, every person and institution, civil government included, must answer to someone because those who rule represent a superior sovereign: children to parents (who represent God and are accountable to Him), students to teachers (who represent parents), employees to employers (who represent consumers),[1] citizens to magistrates (who represent God) in civil government ("able men *who fear God*": Exodus 18:21),[2] and magistrates must answer to the citizenry (who also represent God as self-governors under His sovereignty) at the voting booth (Deuteronomy 1:13). Of course, we all must answer to God "as those who will give an account" (Hebrews 13:17).

Accountability in government (not just civil) is found in a number of places in Scripture. Someone is always reporting to representatives of sovereignty (e.g., Matthew 10:1; Mark 6:7; Luke 7:8; 10:19; 19:17; John 5:27, 30; 19:11; 1 Timothy 3:1-7). This is true even within the Godhead in Jesus' role as mediator: "But I want you to understand that Christ is the head of every man, and the man is the head of a woman, and God is the head of Christ" (1 Corinthians 11:3; cf. 3:23).

Exodus 18 is a lesson in decentralized politics and is especially appropriate in showing the nature of representation and accountability in the area of civil government and the relationship between self-government, family government, and civil government. Moses was given legitimate authority to rule (sovereignty), but he was unable, because of built-in creaturely limitations, to rule effectively and absolutely. Jethro, Moses' father-in-law, gave the following advice to Moses: Put others in leadership positions under you as representatives and make them accountable to you, and the people accountable to their new rulers.

> The thing that you do is not good. You will surely wear out, both yourself and these people who are with you, for the task is too heavy for you; you cannot do it alone. Now listen to me: I shall give you counsel, and God be with you. You be the people's representative before God, and you bring the disputes to God, then teach them the statutes and the laws, and make known to them the way they are to do. Furthermore, you shall select out of all the people able men who fear God, men of truth, those who hate dishonest gain; and you shall place these over them, as leaders of thousands, of hundreds, of fifties and of tens. And let them judge the people at all times; and let it be that every major dispute they will bring to you, but every minor

dispute they themselves will judge. So it will be easier for you, and they will bear the burden with you. If you do this thing and God so commands you, then you will be able to endure, and all these people also will go to their place in peace (Exodus 18:17-23).

Lesser magistrates were appointed with ethical considerations in mind. They were to be "able men who fear God, men of truth, those who hate dishonest gain." Each of these magistrates was responsible to the next higher magistrate: Magistrates over tens were accountable to magistrates over fifties; magistrates over fifties were accountable to magistrates over hundreds; magistrates over hundreds were accountable to magistrates over thousands; and magistrates over thousands were accountable to Moses who was accountable to God. Why the accountability? Because magistrates *represent* God in some way, similar to the way Aaron represented Moses to the people and the way rulers are described in Psalm 82, they are often accorded great honor by being given the lofty title of "god" (*elohim*).

> Then the anger of the LORD burned against Moses, and He said, "Is there not your brother Aaron the Levite? I know that he speaks fluently. And moreover, behold, he is coming out to meet you; when he sees you, he will be glad in his heart. And you are to speak to him and put the words in his mouth; and I, even I, will be with your mouth and his mouth, and I will teach you what you are to do. Moreover, *he shall speak for you to the people; and it shall come about that he shall be as a mouth for you, and you shall be as God to him*" (Exodus 4:14-17; cf. Psalm 82:1, 6; John 10:34).

The Hebrew term for "gods" (*elohim*) in Psalm 82:6, for example, is a reference to those who *exercise judicial authority in God's name*. "The passage refers to the judges of Israel, and the expression 'gods' is applied to them in the exercise of their high and God-given office."[3] To be brought before a judge was like being brought before God, because the judge *represented* God. The word translated "God" in Exodus 21:6 (from the Hebrew *elohim*) is referring to a judge who acts in God's name. This can be seen in Exodus 22:8-9. The word translated "judge" is actually *elohim*, God.

The best men are to rule for the public good founded upon law, thus, a republican form of government. God has ordained governmental "powers" (plural) (Romans 13:1). These "powers" are represented by men who are "ministers of God" (v. 3) This is why Scripture informs us that it is "in the *abundance* of counselors [that] there is deliverance" (Proverbs 11:14b; 24:6).

3. Law: A Moral Code by which to Rule

All governments follow an ethical code (**law**). That ethical code may be perverse or righteous, but an ethical code exists, nevertheless. A perverse ethical code stipulates, for example, that women have a fundamental right to abort their unborn children. A righteous ethical code would protect the unborn (Exodus 21:22-25). The civil magistrate is to render judgment in terms of what is "good" and what is "evil" (Romans 13:3-4). These ethical designations ("good" and "evil") are God's. Rulers at all governmental levels must seek out God's laws and apply them to their appropriate jurisdictions: family laws to the household, ecclesiastical laws to the church, and civil laws to the public sphere as they relate to civil matters.

All citizens and nations are obligated to follow God's laws as they pertain to individuals in self-government, family members in family government, church members in church government, and citizens in civil government. No person is exempt. The *stranger*, an individual *outside* the covenant community of Israel but living under Israel's jurisdiction, was required to obey the law as it was given by God to Moses: "There shall be *one standard* for you; *it shall be for the stranger as well as the native*, for I am the LORD your God" (Leviticus 24:22; cf. Numbers 15:16; Deuteronomy 1:16-17). Belshazzar, a Gentile who was not under the jurisdiction of the Israeli state, broke specific laws from the Mosaic legislation relating to idolatry and was punished for it (Daniel 5). A similar fate happened to Herod under the New Covenant (Acts 12:20-23).

There are those in our day who do not want to hear of man's duty, either personally or civilly, to keep the whole law of God.

It is characteristic of unbelievers to rage against Jehovah and His anointed King, wishing to cast off any bonds of political servitude to Jesus Christ. Psalm 2 explicitly tells us as much (verses 1-6). The gospels illustrate this same political rage. The chief priests bolstered the crowd's demand for the crucifixion of Jesus Christ by insisting "We have no king but Caesar" (John 19:15). The Apostle Paul's experience points to this same political fury. He taught that Jesus was "King of kings" (1 Timothy 6:15) — the primary political king under whom all earthly leaders, "the powers that be," are ordained as "ministers of God" (Romans 13:1-7). For this viewpoint he was run out of Thessalonica, daring to teach "contrary to the decree of Caesar" by saying "that there is another king, Jesus" (Acts 17:7).[4]

Another king means another law. The citizenry knew this. Instead of doing homage to Caesar, they would have to "do homage to the Son" or "perish in the way" (Psalm 2:12). Caesar, too, eventually understood the implications of Jesus' government over all of life. In time, as predicted by God in Daniel 2:40-45, the Roman empire would eventually fall as God's kingdom advanced.

No magistrate is exempt from the demands of God's law. Even rulers outside of Israel were to hear and heed the law of God. In fact, it was David himself who was obligated to "speak of [God's] testimonies before kings" (Psalm 119:46), all the kings of the earth. Such kings are wise when they keep God's law: "By me kings reign, and rulers decree justice. By me princes rule, and nobles, all who judge rightly" (Proverbs 8:15-16). As Paul shows us in Romans 13:3, "rulers are not a cause of fear for good behavior, but for evil."

4. Jurisdiction: Authority to Enforce Sanctions

It is not enough to have a law, there must be legitimacy to enforce the law (sanctions) within specified jurisdictions. God has done this on numerous occasions. The inhabitants of Sodom and Gomorrah were destroyed for breaking God's law against sodomy (Genesis 13:13; 19:4-5; cf. Leviticus 18:22; 20:13). The members of Sodom knew their actions were unlawful, destroying themselves, their families, and the community (cf. Romans 1:18-32). God had made His law known to the world: "Abraham obeyed Me, and kept My charge, My commandments, My statutes, and My laws" (Genesis 26:5; cf. Job 22:22; 23:12). These and other laws were eventually codified, written down for the world to see and learn, after the time of Israel's Exodus (Deuteronomy 4:5-8).

The nations of the world are still obligated to follow God's laws. In our day, sodomy, while still considered a crime in many states, is rarely punished. But "God is not mocked; for whatever a man sows, this he will also reap" (Galatians 6:7). The AIDS virus is a testimony to the Bible's insistence that sanctions are still meted out prior to the final judgment. This shows God's jurisdiction to mete out negative sanctions on rebellion that His God-ordained civil ministers refuse to do.

Families, churches, and civil governments have legitimate authority to enact biblical laws and then to enforce sanctions if those laws are broken. Each government (family, church, and civil) is limited in its authority, however. Parents can only discipline members of their own family, the use of the rod being the most severe form of correction (Proverbs 13:24; 22:15; 23:13; 29:15). Elders can discipline only their church members, excommunication being the most severe form of discipline (Matthew 16:19; 18:15-20; 1 Corinthians 6:1-11). The State has a duty to punish criminal acts that are *civil* in nature, the most severe being execution for capital crimes (Genesis 9:6-7; Exodus 21:12-14; Romans 13:4; 1 Peter 2:14). These are temporal sanctions.

5. Continuity: Stability of Government

The historical landscape is replete with the strewn corpses of fallen dynasties and collapsed kingdoms. There is a reason for this. Every kingdom that has fallen in some way or another has transgressed God's commandments. They either collapsed under the weight of their own decadence or they were conquered by other hostile kingdoms (Daniel 1:17; 2:31-45; 4:28-37; 5:1-31). In either case, the reason for their collapse is ethical: They transgressed God's commandments and God judged them. Such acts of disobedience have repercussions for the continuity of nations and kingdoms. Nations that submit to God remain; those that rebel are judged. This was God's message for Jonah to take to Nineveh: "Arise, go to Nineveh the great city, and cry against it, for their wickedness has come up before Me" (Jonah 1:2; 3:1). The repentance of the Ninevites spared the nation (3:5-10).

During Israel's occupation of the land of Canaan, God made it clear that the reason the previous occupants of the land were evicted was due to their violation of His law (Leviticus 18:24-27). The Canaanites' refusal to obey God's law meant their removal from the land. They were dispossessed because of rebellion. This is why the Psalmist, using God's law as a standard, could assent to God removing "all the wicked of the earth" (Psalm 119:118-119).

There is a cause and effect relationship between obedience or disobedience and God's law. Obedience brings blessing (positive sanctions: Deuteronomy 28:1-14) and disobedience brings cursing (negative sanctions: Deuteronomy 28:15-68). The New Testament confirms this truth:

For rulers are not a cause of fear for good behavior, but for evil. Do you want to have no fear of authority? Do what is good, and you will have praise from the same [positive sanctions/blessing]; for it is a minister of God to you for good [positive sanctions/blessing]. But if you do what is evil, be afraid [negative sanctions/cursing]; for it does not bear the sword for nothing; for it is a minister of God, an avenger who brings wrath [negative sanctions/cursing] upon the one who practices evil (Romans 13:3-4).

"Righteousness exalts a nation [positive sanctions/blessing], but sin is a disgrace to any people [negative sanctions/cursing]" (Proverbs 14:34).

During the period of the Judges, Israel's failure to heed God's warnings regarding His law brought judgment and temporary displacement from the full use of their land inheritance (Judges 6:1). As time went on, Israel slowly lost its inheritance through repeated acts of rebellion (Jeremiah 25:1-11). Eventually the entire nation was exiled for seventy years and came under God's righteous sanctions (Daniel 9:11-16). One final act of rebellion, the rejection of the promised Messiah, meant disinheritance: "Therefore I say to you, the kingdom of God will be taken away from you, and be given to a nation producing the fruit of it" (Matthew 21:43; cf. 23:38).

The principle of continuity affects all governments. Obedience brings blessing (inheritance/continuity), while disobedience brings cursing (disinheritance/discontinuity). This clearly can be seen in family government:

> Children, obey your parents in the Lord, for this is right. Honor your father and mother (which is the first commandment with a promise), "that it may be well with you, *and that you may live long on the earth*" (Ephesians 6:1-3).

This is why Scripture tells parents to teach God's laws and commands to their children "that the generation to come might know, even the children yet to be born, that they may arise and tell them to their children, that they should put their confidence in God, and not forget the works of God, but keep His commandments" (Psalm 78:6-8).

---

[1]In a free-market economic system consumers are ultimately sovereign.

[2]There is no "divine right of kings." Although elected officials represent God, they do not do so autonomously. If a magistrate could claim a divine right, then there would be no need for him to "fear God."

[3]Leon Morris, *The Gospel According to John* (Grand Rapids, MI: Eerdmans, 1971), p. 525.

[4]Greg L. Bahnsen, "What Kind of Morality Should We Legislate?," *The Biblical Worldview* (October, 1988), pp. 5-6.

Books for Further Reading and Study

The purpose of the *God and Government* textbook series is to give Christians an overview of what the Bible says about government, particularly civil government. The *God and Government* textbook series was not designed to answer all the questions raised regarding the function and purpose of civil government. In order to take the student further in his or her study, a list of books and newsletters has been provided covering a variety of topics relating to this study. A number of these books are out of print. I have included a list of out-of-print book services that can assist you in locating them for your library.

I. Christian Heritage

Verna M. Hall and Rosalie J. Slater have spent many years researching America's Christian history. Their works contain copies of original documents dealing with our nation's founding. The first five books listed below may be ordered directly from The Foundation for American Christian Education (FACE), P.O. Box 27035, San Francisco, CA 94127.

A number of books not listed in this section but included under other headings have a wealth of historical material related to the topic of Christian history.

The Christian History of the Constitution of the United States of America (FACE)

The Christian History of the Constitution of the United State of America: Christian Self-Government with Union (FACE)

Teaching and Learning America's Christian History (FACE)

The Christian History of the American Revolution (FACE)

American Dictionary of the English Language, by Noah Webster (1828) (FACE). Facsimile Edition 1967. This reprint gives the meanings of words as they were used in the eighteenth century. Very helpful in understanding historical documents.

Ahlstrom, Sydney E. *A Religious History of the American People.* 2 Vols. Garden City, NY: Doubleday, 1975. An important work on America's religious history particularly since it establishes the overwhelmingly Christian origins of the American people at the time of the War of Independence.

Amos, Gary. *Defending the Declaration: How the Bible and Christianity Influenced the Writing of the Declaration of Independence.* Brentwood, TN: Wolgemuth & Hyatt, 1989. Ten years of research have gone into this book by a Christian lawyer and professor of law and government. The author disputes the assertion that there was almost no Christian influence on the minds and writings of America's forefathers. Extensively documented from primary and secondary sources. Includes a comprehensive bibliography.

Bradford, M. E. *A Worthy Company: The Dramatic Story of the Men Who Founded Our Country*. Westchester, IL: Crossway Books (1982), 1988. An excellent, well-researched biographical work on the framers of the Constitution claiming that nearly all the Representatives were Bible-believing Christians (50 of the 55 Framers).

Campbell, Tim J. *Central Themes of American Life*. Grand Rapids, MI: Eerdmans, 1959. Deals with the hand of God in United States history, the main tenets of American civil government, economic life, religious liberty, and other Christian themes central to American culture and life.

DeMar, Gary. "The Christian Origins of American Civil Government," in *Ruler of the Nations: Biblical Principles of Government*. Atlanta, GA: American Vision, 1987. This appendix to *Ruler of the Nations* presents an overview of America's theological beginnings. Includes some of the young nation's first governing documents and the biblical principles that gave them stability.

_____. "The Theonomic Response to National Confessionalism," in Gary Scott Smith, ed., *God and Politics: Four Views on the Reformation of Civil Government*. Phillipsburg, NJ: Presbyterian and Reformed, 1989. Defines what is meant by America being a "Christian nation." Contains original source material showing America's biblical origins: official pronouncements and declarations, state constitutions, and assessments by well respected historians.

Draper, James T. and Forrest E. Watson. *If the Foundations be Destroyed*. Nashville, TN: Thomas Nelson, 1984. An historical survey of America's biblical heritage and how it was lost.

Eidsmoe, John. *Christianity and the Constitution: The Faith of Our Founding Fathers*. Grand Rapids, MI: Baker Book House, 1987. The author meticulously documents his position that many of the Founding Fathers were Christians, using the writings of the Founders themselves, records of their conversations, and accounts of activities related to their contemporaries. The first four chapters deal with major influences that affected the Founding Fathers: Calvinism, deism, freemasonry, and science. The influence of political thinkers such as Blackstone, John Locke, and Montesquieu are also presented. The following chapters deal with thirteen Founding Fathers, from Witherspoon to Pickney.

Hart, Benjamin. *Faith and Freedom: The Christian Roots of American Liberty*. San Bernardino, CA: Here's Life Publishers, 1988. What does the past tell us about America's founding? Was America founded on secular principles, or did the Christian religion, from the landing of the Pilgrims to the drafting of the Constitution, lay a deep foundation of governmental values and principles? Hart asserts that without Christianity there can be no true freedom. America is free because of its Christian beginnings.

LaHaye, Tim. *Faith of Our Founding Fathers*. Brentwood, TN: Wolgemuth & Hyatt, 1987. An interesting historical work that shows the theological context out of which our nation grew. A series of brief but informative biographies of the most influential Founding Fathers is included. In addition, there is a study of the outstanding Christians among the Founding Fathers. Great ammunition to use against those who disparage the Christian beginnings of America.

Marshall, Peter and David Manuel. *From Sea to Shining Sea*. Old Tappan, NJ: Fleming H. Revell, 1986. A continuation of the story begun in *The Light and the Glory*.

—————. *The Light and the Glory*. Old Tappan, NJ: Fleming H. Revell, 1977. A popularly written and well researched book (although not footnoted) on God's plan for America. Enjoyable reading.

Morris, B. F. *The Christian Character of the Civil Institutions of the United States*. Philadelphia, PA: G. W. Childs, 1964. A long out-of-print work that contains a staggering amount of original source material that shows America was began as a Christian nation.

North, Gary, ed. *The Journal of Christian Reconstruction*. (Chalcedon, P.O. Box 158, Vallecito, CA 95251). Provides a wealth of material on many topics of importance for those Christian who are looking for a scholarly approach to biblical and historical studies. Some issues which are of particular historical importance are listed below:

Symposium on Biblical Law. Vol II, No.2, Winter, 1975-76.

Symposium on Christianity and the American Revolution. Vol. III, No. 1, Summer, 1976.

Symposium on Politics. Vol. V, No. 1, Summer, 1978.

Symposium on Puritanism and Law. Vol. V, No. 2, Winter, 1979.

Symposium on Puritanism and Progress. Vol. VI, No. 1, Summer, 1979.

Symposium on Puritanism and Society. Vol. VI, No. 2, Winter, 1979-80.

Singer, C. Gregg. *A Theological Interpretation of American History*. Nutley, NJ: The Craig Press, 1981 (Revised Edition). Analysis of the intellectual mainsprings of American thought and history, particularly the impact of non-Christian philosophies on American institutions.

Stout, Harry S. *The New England Soul: Preaching and Religious Culture in Colonial New England*. New York: Oxford University Press, 1986. A fascinating study of the role clergymen played in educating the church-going masses of the time. Stout asserts that the Puritan sermon was the only regular voice of authority for the colonies and, as such, provides a broad picture of the ideological foundations of the American Revolution.

II. Theological and Historical Foundations

Bandow, Doug. *Beyond Good Intentions: A Biblical View of Politics.* Westchester, IL: Crossway Books, 1988. A comprehensive but somewhat uneven approach to a biblical theory of politics. Loaded with biblical references and historical sources.

Brown, Harold O.J. *The Reconstruction of the Republic.* Milford, MI: Mott Media, (1977) 1981. A leading evangelical scholar shows how Christian withdrawal from public life has created a moral and spiritual vacuum that is being filled by groups hostile to biblical principles. Suggests ways to recover our biblical heritage.

Bulman, James D. *It Is Their Right: The Declaration of Independence and What Has Followed.* Greensboro, NC: Gateway Publications, 1975. A states' rights interpretation of the Declaration. Powerful chapter on "Religious Concepts in Our Fundamental Documents."

Culver, Robert Duncan. *Toward a Biblical View of Civil Government.* Chicago, IL: Moody Press, 1974. Deals with the biblical concept of civil government from Old and New Testament sources. A very interesting analysis of some difficult Scripture passages.

Eidsmoe, John. *God and Caesar: Christian Faith and Political Action.* A comprehensive guide showing the duty Christians owe to the State in terms of their relationship to God and the Scriptures. Covers such topics as church/state relations, the family, crime and punishment, education, censorship and pornography, civil disobedience, liberation theology, and military service.

Hamilton, Alexander, et al. *The Federalist.* Middletown, CT: Wesleyan University Press, 1961. Essays first printed in several New York newspapers during the fall and winter of 1787-1788 dealing with the then proposed Constitution. Indispensable reading for a proper understanding of the arguments used by those who worked for the Constitution's ratification.

Rushdoony, R. J. *The Foundations of Social Order: Studies in the Creeds and Councils of the Early Church.* Philadelphia, PA: Presbyterian and Reformed, 1972. Illustrates how Western freedoms developed from basic Christian doctrines.

_____. *This Independent Republic: Studies in the Nature and Meaning of American History.* Nutley, NJ: The Craig Press, 1964. Examines our Christian political heritage, especially in the area of law.

_____. *The Nature of the American System.* Nutley, NJ: The Craig Press, 1965. Argues that limited government is based on biblical principles and that modern liberalism has attempted to replace it with a god-like, monolithic state having unlimited powers.

_____. *Politics of Guilt and Pity.* Nutley, NJ: The Craig Press, 1970. Because unregenerate men are dominated by sin and guilt, they are easily manipulated by those who advocate an expansionistic central government to rid mankind of social ills.

Walton, Rus. *One Nation Under God*. Nashville, TN: Thomas Nelson, (1975) 1987. Sets forth biblical principles for government, economics, education, and the family and shows how socialism and humanism are undermining these principles in America today. A study guide is included.

III. Christian Social Action

DeMar, Gary. *Ruler of the Nations: Biblical Blueprints for Government*. Atlanta, GA: American Vision, 1985. While this volume sets forth a biblical rationale for government, three chapters are devoted to practical matters relating to family, church, and civil governments.

_____. *"You've Heard It Said."* Ft. Worth, TX: Dominion Press, 1990. Many Christians will not involve themselves in what they consider to be "worldly matters." They often recite reasons like politics is dirty, Jesus didn't get mixed up in politics, Jesus' kingdom is not of this world, and many more. This book answers twenty five common objections to Christian activism.

North, Gary, ed. *The Journal of Christian Reconstruction*, Symposium on Social Action, 1981, Vol. VIII, No. 1. A series of articles that deal with the biblical concept of social action. Shows how "Christian Socialism" is out of accord with Scripture as a way of solving society's ills.

Thoburn, Robert L. *The Christian and Politics*. A very helpful book written by an ordained minister who holds three academic degrees, started three home mission churches, founded the Fairfax Christian School in Fairfax, Virginia, and served as a member of the Virginia House of Delegates from 1978-1980. This small book presents a biblical and practical rationale for Christian involvement in the civil sphere of government. Answers many of the objections raised by Christian activism critics.

IV. Church/State Issues

Eidsmoe, John. *The Christian Legal Advisor*. Grand Rapids, MI: Baker Book House, (1984) 1987. A massive volume (nearly 600 pages) written by a lawyer and pastor for other lawyers and pastors, teachers, and anyone interested in the law and how it should be applied from a biblical perspective. Eidsmoe avoids confusing legal jargon and terminology. Part one is an introduction to biblical principles of law and their application to modern society. Part two explains the background and meaning of the First Amendment and other constitutional protections of particular interest to Christians. Part three deals with the practical legal problems involving churches and the ministry, as well as individual Christians. A very practical book.

Kik, J. Marcellus. *Church and State: The Story of Two Kingdoms*. New York, NY: Thomas Nelson and Sons, 1963. Traces the Church's conflict with the State biblically and historically.

210

_____. *The Supreme Court and Prayer in the Public Schools*. Philadelphia, PA: Presbyterian and Reformed, 1963. Discusses the Court's infamous decision.

O'Neill, J. M. *Religion and Education Under the Constitution*. New York, NY: Harper and Brothers, 1949. An analysis of court decisions interpreting the historic intent of the Constitution on the separation of Church and State. A wealth of historical information.

IV. First Amendment Issues

Buzzard, Lynn. R. and Samuel Ericsson. *The Battle for Religious Liberty*. Elgin, IL: David C. Cook, 1982. A popular exposition of the First Amendment by two Christian lawyers. This helpful book outlines the rights of citizens as they relate to education, personal liberties, and religious ministries.

Cord, Robert L. *The Separation of Church and State: Historical Fact and Current Fiction*. Grand Rapids, MI: Baker Book House, (1982) 1988. What's the real story behind the meaning of the First Amendment? Most argue that the Amendment was designed to erect a "high and impregnable" wall between church and state. Of course, this has come to mean between religion and state. *The Separation of Church and State* disputes this thesis, and shows, through this thoroughly researched book that the First Amendment was designed to protect state religious establishments.

Dreisbach, Daniel L. *Real Threat and Mere Shadow: Religious Liberty and the First Amendment*. Westchester, IL: Crossway Books, 1987. An extensive study of the First Amendment showing how the Amendment has been wrongly interpreted and ridiculously applied.

Whitehead, John W. *The Second American Revolution*. Westchester, IL: Crossway Books, (1982) 1985. The Supreme Court is the Constitution's interpreter. This is a power it has claimed for itself, and, unfortunately, most politicians and voters have accepted the Court's view. Lawyer John Whitehead, president of the Rutherford Institute, an organization that aggressively defends the First Amendment's protection of religious rights, traces the sordid history of the displacement of the Amendment's original purpose. The book follows the practical implications of what this knew definition has done to our nation.

_____. *The Separation Illusion*. Milford, MI: Mott Media, 1977. Shows the impossibility of separating God from Civil government. Dispels the idea of "separation of Church and State" as popularly interpreted today. Sets forth the true intent and meaning of the First Amendment. Must reading!

IV. Law

Bahnsen, Greg L. *By This Standard: The Authority of God's Law Today*. Tyler, TX: Institute for Christian Economics, 1985. Are Christians free to be lawless? All

Christians would say no. But what is the relationship between God's law and the Christian? How much of it is the Christian (and the world) bound to obey? This volume will help you answer these questions.

_____. *Theonomy in Christian Ethics*. Nutley, NJ: The Craig Press, 1977. A rigorous biblical, historical, and logical defense of the applicability of the law of God for all ages and cultures.

Davis, John Jefferson. *Evangelical Ethics: Issues Facing the Church Today*. Phillipsburg, NJ: Presbyterian and Reformed, 1985. While dealing with an full range of ethical topics (contraception, divorce and remarriage, homosexuality, abortion, infanticide, etc.), the chapters on capital punishment, civil disobedience and revolution, and war and peace are penitent to the topics outlined in this volume of *God and Government*.

Ingram, T. Robert. *The World Under God's Law: Criminal Aspects of the Welfare State*. Houston, TX: St. Thomas Press, 1962. A study of the social implications of the Ten Commandments. Shows how biblical concepts are embodied in our legal system and how humanists and socialists are attempting to modify that system to reflect their own religious beliefs.

Laski, Harold J., ed. *A Defense of Liberty Against Tyrants*. Gloucester, MA: Peter Smith, (1942) 1963. The classic French Protestant defense of revolution against tyrants which did much to influence the founding fathers in their defense of revolution against the tyrannical practices of King George III. Written a century before John Locke in 1579. John Adams said that it was one of the most influential books in America on the eve of the revolution.

Rushdoony, Rousas John. *Institutes of Biblical Law*. Nutley, NJ: The Craig Press, 1972. A thorough study of biblical law as a standard for the ordering of human society. An important tool in any Christian reconstruction effort.

_____. *Law and Liberty*. Fairfax, VA: Thoburn Press, 1977. These essays were originally delivered as a series of radio addresses in 1966 and 1967, over several stations from coast to coast. Can be considered either a distillation or an introductory summary of the *Institutes of Biblical Law*. Written for a popular audience and is an excellent introduction to all of Rushdoony's works.

Rutherford, Samuel. *Lex Rex, or The Law and the Prince*. Harrisonburg, VA: Sprinkle Publications, 1980. A Facsimile reprint of a very influential work which did much to influence the thinking of those who participated in the War of Independence. Rutherford maintains that even the king is under law. Develops a theology of resistance against tyrants.

Sproul, R. C. "The Christian and Government: What to Do when Uncle Sam Wants You," in *Lifeviews: Understanding the Ideas That Shape Society Today*. Old Tappan, NJ: Fleming H. Revell, 1986. A basic overview of the Christian's role in government. A good place to start for beginners.

V. Political Structures and the Constitution

Bales, James D. *Communism: Its Faith and Fallacies.* Grand Rapids, MI: Baker Book House, 1962. An exposition and criticism of Communism. A review of the philosophy of Communism, the concept of class and class struggle, the Communist attitude toward religion, and the Communist objective of final destruction of religion.

Conley, Patrick T. and John P. Kaminski. *The Constitution and the States: The Role of the Original Thirteen in the Framing and Adoption of the Federal Constitution.* Madison, WI: Madison House, 1988. The Constitution had to go through a ratification process. This process was not done by popular vote. The thirteen sovereign states, which sent delegates to the national Convention, were the ratifying agents. This volumes outlines the process of ratification that came through the states. Nicely illustrated with engravings and maps.

DeKoster, Lester. *Communism and the Christian Faith.* Grand Rapids, MI: Eerdmans Publishing, 1962. "A concise guide to the fundamentals of Communism, a pointed contrast between communist and Christian faith, and a clear call to Christian social action."

Kaminski, John P. and Richard Leffler. *Federalists and Antifederalists: The Debate Over the Ratification of the Constitution.* Madison, WI: Madison House, 1989. Many Americans are familiar with the Federalist Papers, a series of articles designed to support the ratification of the new Constitution. Little is read of the *antifederalists,* those who believed that the new Constitution took too much power from the states and created a central government with the potential of wielding unlimited power. This volume provides an overview of the wide ranging debate on the ratification of the Constitution.

Lee, Francis Nigel. *Communist Eschatology.* Nutley, NJ: The Craig Press, 1973. The definitive work on the goals of the communistic faith. Deals with all aspects of communistic thought and the way it permeates every area of life. Develops a Christian strategy for world-wide dominion.

House, H. Wayne, ed., *Restoring the Constitution: 1787-1987.* Chicago, IL: Moody Press, (1987) 1989. A series of essays from a number of constitutional scholars and legal activists that seek to pay proper tribute to the Constitution, the document upon which our Republic rests.

Hubbard, Bela. *Political and Economic Structures.* Caldwell, ID: The Caxton Printers, Ltd., 1964. A handy reference work which defines ancient and modern political and economic structures. Also deals with the United States Constitution and the First Amendment.

McDonald, Forest. *Novus Ordo Seclorum: The Intellectual Origins of the Constitution.* Lawrence, KS: University Press of Kansas, 1985. This volume completes a trilogy of sorts for McDonald. *We the People* (1958) countered Beard's economic analysis of the

Constitution, while McDonald's *E Pluribus Unum* discussed the "sophisticated picture of the dynamic interrelationships of avarice and American politics" at both the national and state level. *Novus Ordo Seclorum* describes the intellectual dimension: What were the sources of their ideas?

North, Gary. *Political Polytheism: The Myth of Pluralism* (Tyler, TX: Institute for Christian Economics, 1989). While this book deals with the issue of "pluralism," there is a very informative section (Part 3) addressing the nature of the commitment of the Founders to a consistent biblical world view.

The three-volume GOD AND GOVERNMENT series is just one of the many superb Christian educational products available from American Vision.

American Vision is a non-profit Christian educational organization that is a unique presence in today's Christian culture. American Vision believes and proclaims the message that God's Word is the standard for all of life. The Bible is the ultimate authority for questions concerning government, law, business, economics, family, ethics, the arts, science, and every other area of life.

American Vision presents its message through books, audio and video tapes, seminars, radio and television media, a monthly magazine, and personal presentations.

Bibliography

Boice, James M. *God and History*. Downers Grove, IL: Inter-Varsity Press, 1981.

Bradford, William. *History of Plymouth Plantation: 1606-1646*, William T. Davis, ed. New York: Charles Scribner's Sons, 1908.

Burleigh, Joseph Barlett. *The American Manual*. Philadelphia, PA: Lippencott, Grambo & Co., 1852.

Calvin, John. *Commentary on a Harmony of the Evangelists, Matthew, Mark, and Luke*, Vol. 3. Grand Rapids, MI: Baker Book House, reprinted 1990.

_____. *Institutes of the Christian Religion*. John T. McNeill, ed. Philadelphia, PA: Westminster Press, 1960.

Chilton, David. *Productive Christians in an Age of Guilt Manipulators*. Tyler, TX: Institute for Christian Economics, 1981.

Dabney, Robert L. *Lectures in Systematic Theology*. Grand Rapids, MI: Zondervan Publishing House, (1878) 1972.

_____. *Discussions Philosophical*. Vallecito, CA: Ross House Books, (1892) 1980.

Hayek, Friedrich A. *The Constitution of Liberty*. Chicago, IL: The University of Chicago Press, 1960.

Henry, Patrick, in Jonathan Elliot, ed. *The Debates in the Several State Conventions on the Adoption of the Federal Constitution as Recommended by the General Convention at Philadelphia in 1787*, Vol 3. Philadelphia, PA: Lippencott, (1836) 1907.

Hodge, Archibald A. *Commentary on the Confession of Faith*. Philadelphia, PA: Presbyterian Board of Publications, 1869.

_____. *Evangelical Theology*. Carlisle, PA: The Banner of Truth Trust, (1873) 1977.

Hodge, Charles. *A Commentary on Romans*. Carlisle, PA: The Banner of Truth Trust, (1864) 1972.

Kramer, Rita. *In Defense of the Family: Raising Children in America Today*. New York: Basic Books, 1983.

Lee, Francis Nigel. *Human Social Relationships*. Memphis, TN: Christian Studies Center, no date. An unpublished work.

_____. *Man and His Culture*. Memphis, TN: Christian Studies Center, no date. An unpublished work.

Morecraft, Joseph C. *The Keys and the Sword*. (Chalcedon Presbyterian Church, P.O. Box 888022, Atlanta, GA 30338, no date). An unpublished work.

Walter A. Maier. *For Better, Not for Worse.* St. Louis, MO: Concordia, 1933.

Morris, Henry. *The Genesis Record.* Grand Rapids, MI: Baker Book House, 1976.

Morris, Leon. *The Gospel According to John.* Grand Rapids, MI: Eerdmans, 1971.

Morton, R. Kemp, *God in the Constitution.* Nashville, TN: Cokesbury Press, 1933.

North, Gary. *Successful Investing in an Age of Envy.* Sheridan, IN: Steadman Press, 1981.

_____. *Unconditional Surrender: God's Program for Victory.* Tyler, TX: Institute for Christian Economics, 1983.

Roehrs, Walter H. and Martin H. Franzmann. *Concordia Self-Study Commentary.* St. Louis, MO: Concordia, 1979.

Rushdoony, Rousas J. *Thy Kingdom Come.* Fairfax, VA: Thoburn Press, 1970.

Palmer, Benjamin M. *The Family in its Civil and Churchly Aspects: An Essay in Two Parts.* Harrisonburg, VA: (1876) 1981.

Schaeffer, Francis A. *Genesis in Space and Time.* Downers Grove, IL: Inter-Varsity Press, 1972.

_____. *The Church at the End of the 20th Century.* Downers Grove, IL: Inter-Varsity Press, 1970.

Schaeffer, Franky. *Addicted to Mediocrity.* Westchester, IL: Cornerstone Books, 1981.

Stokes, Anson Phelps and Leo Pfeffer, *Church and State in the United States.* New York: Harper & Row, (1950) 1964.

Toffler, Alvin. *The Third Wave.* New York: William Morrow and Company, 1980.

Thornwell, James H. *The Collected Writings of James Henley Thornwell.* Vols. 1 and 4. Carlisle, PA: Banner of Truth Trust (1873), 1974.

Upshur, Abel P. *The Federal Government: Its Nature and Character; Being a Review of Judge Story's Commentaries on the Constitution of the United States.* New York: Van Evrie, Horton & Co., 1868.

Wines, E. C. *The Hebrew Republic.* Uxbridge, MA: American Presbyterian Press, no date.

Picture Credits

Cover

Embarkation of the Pilgrims (detail). National Geographic Society Photographer. U.S. Capitol Historical Society, Washington, D.C.

Introduction

Lesson 1

Lesson 8

Lesson 9

About American Vision

AMERICAN VISION IS A CHRISTIAN EDUCATIONAL ORGANIZATION which is filling a unique place in today's Christian community. The purpose of American Vision is to help Christians understand their lives and their world in light of Scripture. American Vision publishes books and magazines, arranges seminars and debates, and produces a wide range of other materials to proclaim Christ's authority over all of life.

To place an order or to receive information, please contact:

AMERICAN VISION
P.O. BOX 220
POWDER SPRINGS, GA 30127

Toll free (Orders Only Please): 800-628-9460
Business Offices: 770-222-7266
Fax: 770-222-7269

Web Sites: www.americanvision.org